A Sourcebook about Music

The Sourcebook Series:

A Sourcebook about Music

Compiled by
Alan J. Hommerding
Diana Kodner

LITURGY
TRAINING
PUBLICATIONS

Acknowledgments

We are grateful to the many authors and publishers who have given permission to include their work. Every effort has been made to determine the ownership of all texts and to make proper arrangements for their use. Any oversight that may have occurred, if brought to our attention, will gladly be corrected in future editions. The many people who contributed to this book are named in the Introduction.

Acknowledgments will be found in the Notes. Permission to reprint any texts in this book must be obtained from the copyright owners.

Acquisitions editor: Diana Kodner
Production editor: Audrey Novak Riley
Permissions editor: Theresa Houston
Editorial assistance: Lorraine Schmidt
Production: Lisa Buckley
Production artist: James Mellody-Pizzato
Series design format: Michael Tapia

Printed in the United States of America

04 03 02 01 00 99 98 97   6 5 4 3 2 1

ISBN 1-56854-153-8
MUSISB

Contents

Introduction

When Alan Hommerding and I first discussed the scope and content of this collection, it became clear that there was no single obvious approach to take. Most of the people who have contributed their cherished quotes to this book are liturgical ministers. Naturally, this provides a kind of focus — one that never strays far from God. But musicians and liturgists are an opinionated and contentious lot. Some prefer the passionate and the sensual, while others strive for simplicity and "pure spirit." We would be hard pressed to arrive at a definition of music that all could ascribe to. Are notes on a page music? Is the song of a bird music?

Much of what you will read in this anthology appears contradictory. The perception of a piece of music is a very personal experience, yet "anyone with ears to hear" shares in the experience, and consequently, has an opinion. Perhaps it is the contradictions that provide for creativity and diversity. The tensions are a metaphor for the greater human struggle to bring about the reign of God. With this understanding, conflicting quotes are at times deliberately brought together. For example, while the famous excerpt from Ecclesiastes tells us that there is nothing new under the sun, others excitedly explore future possibilities for music-making. Throughout, there is the juxtaposition of the personal with the communal and the human with the divine.

Still, this is not a comprehensive collection of quotes about music. It is, rather, a collection of beloved texts from the storehouses of a small yet diverse group of musicians and liturgists. A conscious effort has been made to keep this book in the style of LTP's other *Sourcebooks*. We have drawn from poetry, fiction, sacred song and scripture, as well as from the thoughts of composers, performers, church leaders, musicologists and philosophers, eastern and western, ancient and modern.

The following people must be thanked for their contributions to this book: Bob Batastini, Marcia Berry, David Cinquegrani, CP, Chris Comella, Kelly Dobbs-Mickus, Dorothy Dwight, BVM, William Ferris, Edward Foley, CAP, Nick Freund, Robert A. Harris, Mike Hay, Ted Heppner, Kathleen Hughes, RSCJ, Robert M. Hutmacher, OFM, Steve Janco, J. Michael Joncas,

Mary Beth Kunde-Anderson, Denise LaGiglia, David Larsen, James Marchionda, OP, J. Michael McMahon, John Allyn Melloh, SM, Paul Philibert, OP, David Philippart, Ron Rendek, Victor Sanders, David Seitz, Tom Strickland, Randall Swanson, James Michael Thompson, Vicky Tufano, Mary Louise Van Dyke, Jeffrey Wasson, Scott Weidler and Michael Wustrow.

This book is not meant to be read cover to cover, but there is an implied flow and structure. The music-making discussed herein begins and ends with the oneness of all things, flowing from a loving creator. (Even the self-proclaimed non-believer would likely admit that music can and frequently does lead us to the realm of something greater than ourselves.) It is in this spirit that we offer what Alan has called a banquet of texts.

— Diana Kodner

Singing is the most human, most companionable of the arts. It joins us together in the whole realm of sound, forging a group identity where there were only individuals and making a communicative statement that far transcends what any one of us could do alone. It is a paradigm of union with the creator. It is what the words talk about. We *need* to sing well.

Alice Parker

Without music, life would be an error.

Friedrich Nietzsche
Nineteenth century

Sing the Lord a new song.
Let the sea with its creatures,
the coastland and its people
fill the world with praise.

Let every village and town,
from Kedar on the plain
to Sela in the hills,
take up the joyful song.
Sing glory to the Lord,
give praise across the world.

Isaiah 42:10–12

B UT suddenly from out of the air it seemed a great singing burst forth, voices high and clear and declaring. Tonio felt a catch in his throat. For a second he could not move, his body perfectly rigid as he absorbed the shock of this singing, and then he squirmed, eyes upward, the candles for the moment blinding him. "Be still," said his mother, who could hardly hold him. The singing grew richer, fuller.

It came in waves from either side of the immense nave, melody interwoven with melody. Tonio could almost see it, a great golden net thrown out as if on the lapping sea in shimmering sunlight. The very air teemed with sound. And finally he saw, right above, the singers.

They stood in two huge lofts to the left and right side of the church, mouths open, faces gleaming in reflected light; they appeared like the angels in the mosaics.

In a second, Tonio had dropped to the floor. He felt his mother's hand slip as she went to catch him. He dashed through the press of skirts and cloaks, perfume and winter air, and saw the open door to the stairway.

It seemed the walls around him throbbed with the chords of the organ as he climbed, and suddenly he stood in the warmth of the choir loft itself, among these tall singers.

A little commotion ensued. He was at the very rail and look-ing up into the eyes of a giant of a man whose voice poured out of him as clean and golden as the clarion of the trumpet. The man sang the one great word, "Alleluia!" which had the peculiar sound of a call to someone, a summoning. And all the men behind him picked it up, singing it over and over again at intervals, overlapping one upon the other.

While across the church the other choir returned it in mounting volume.

Tonio opened his mouth. He started singing. He sang the one word right in time with the tall singer and he felt the man's hand close warmly on his shoulder. The singer was nodding to him, he was saying with his large, almost sleepy brown eyes, Yes, sing, without saying it. Tonio felt the man's lean flank beneath his robe, and then an arm wound down about his waist to lift him.

The whole congregation shimmered below, the Doge in his chair of golden cloth, the Senate in their purple robes, coun-cillors in scarlet, all the patricians of Venice in their white wigs, but Tonio's eyes were fixed on the singer's face as he heard his own voice like a bell ringing out distinct from the singer's clarion. Tonio's body went away. He left it, carried out on the air with his voice and the singer's voice as the sounds became indistinguishable. He saw the pleasure in the singer's quivering eyes, that sleepiness lifted. But the pow-erful sound erupting from the man's chest astonished him.   Anne Rice

MUSIC leads us to the threshold of repentance, of unbearable realization of our own vanity and frailty and of the terrible relevance of God. I would define myself as a person who has been smitten by music, as a person who has never recovered from the blows of music. And yet, music is a vessel that may hold anything. It may express vulgarity; it may impart sublimity. It may utter vanity; it may inspire humility. It may engender fury; it may kindle compassion. It may convey stupidity and it can be the voice of grandeur. It often voices man's highest reverence, but often brings to expression frightful arrogance.

Abraham Heschel

THE year 1956 was more meaningful to me as the 200th anniversary of the birth of Wolfgang Amadeus Mozart. And the high point of 1956 for me was my invitation to give the memorial address on Mozart and his work at the celebration held in Basel. I am not especially gifted or cultured artistically and certainly not inclined to confuse or identify the history of salvation with any part of the history of art. But the golden sounds and melodies of Mozart's music have from early times spoken to me not as gospel but as parables of the realm of God's free grace as revealed in the gospel — and they do so again and again with great spontaneity and directness. . . . There are probably few theological study rooms in which pictures of Calvin and Mozart are to be seen hanging next to each other and at the same height.

Karl Barth

Music is a moral law.
It gives soul to the universe,
Wings to the mind,
Flight to the imagination,
A charm to sadness,
Happiness and life to everything.
It is the essence of order
And lends to all that is good
And just and beautiful.

Plato
Fourth century BCE

Nothing is better than music. When it takes us out of time, it has done more for us than we have the right to hope for. It has broadened the limits of our sorrowful lives; it has lit up the sweetness of our hours of happiness by effacing the pettinesses that diminish us, bringing us back pure and new to what was, what will be and what music has created for us.

Nadia Boulanger

I am not satisfied with him who despises music, as all fanatics do; for music is an endowment and a gift of God, not a gift of men. It also drives away the devil and makes people cheerful; one forgets all anger, unchasteness, pride, and other vices. I place music next to theology and give it the highest praise. And we see how David and all saints put their pious thoughts into verse, rhyme, and songs, because music reigns in times of peace.

Martin Luther
Sixteenth century

SIDDHARTHA listened. He was now listening intently, completely absorbed, quite empty, taking in everything. . . . He could no longer distinguish the different voices — the merry voice from the weeping voice, the childish voice from the manly voice. They all belonged to each other. . . . They were all interwoven and interlocked, entwined in a thousand ways. And all the voices, all the goals, all the yearnings, all the sorrows, all the pleasures, all the good and evil, all of them together was the world. All of them together was the stream of events, the music of life . . . when he did not listen to the sorrow or laughter, when he did not bind his soul to any one particular voice and absorb it in his Self, but heard them all, the whole, the unity, then the great song of a thousand voices consisted of one word: Om — perfection.

Hermann Hesse

WE need each other's voice to sing,
    each other's strength to love,
each other's views to help us bring
our hearts to God above.
Our lives like coals placed side by side
to feed each other's flame,
shall with the Spirit's breath provide
a blaze of faith to claim.

We give our alleluias
to the church's common chord:
    Alleluia!
    Alleluia!
Praise, O praise, O praise the Lord!

Thomas H. Troeger

THE treasury of sacred music is to be preserved and culti-
    vated with great care. Choirs must be assiduously devel-
oped, especially in cathedral churches. Bishops and other
pastors of souls must take great care to ensure that whenever
the sacred action is to be accompanied by chant, the whole
body of the faithful may be able to contribute that active
participation which is rightly theirs.

Constitution on the
Sacred Liturgy

WHAT is this place where we are meeting?
Only a house, the earth its floor,
Walls and a roof sheltering people,
Windows for light, an open door.
Yet it becomes a body that lives
When we are gathered here,
And know our God is near.

Words from afar, stars that are falling,
Sparks that are sown in us like seed.
Names for our God, dreams, signs and wonders
Sent from the past are all we need.
We in this place remember and speak
Again what we have heard:
God's free redeeming word.

And we accept bread at his table,
Broken and shared, a living sign.
Here in this world, dying and living,
We are each other's bread and wine.
This is the place where we can receive
What we need to increase:
Huub Oosterhuis   Our justice and God's peace.

B AD music in church is a bad thing. Some of the greatest of all music is church music. The music of the Catholic church [pre – Vatican II] makes one forget self. It is ridiculous to use the pronoun "I" in Chartres Cathedral. There is a revival of church music today. The great ages of mankind have their roots in the spiritual life. It is interesting that many young men today are doing religious music.

Nadia Boulanger

A UGUSTINE'S commentary on Psalm 150 is again espe- cially useful since it gave countless later readers in the West the idea that ensemble sounds could and would join together in praise, which was all the justification musical clergy needed: ". . . so that they sound not singly but together in the most harmonious diversity, as is ordered in *organum*. For the saints too will differ harmoniously, not disharmoniously, from their fellows."

Peter Williams

C ONSIDERING issues of liturgical formation, structures and texts together remind us that no one discipline can be considered apart from the whole. Musicians, architects, liturgists, poets and presiders need to be in conversation. All of these — and a host of others — need to share a vision of worship and common principles that can help to realize this vision.

Milwaukee Symposia for Church Composers

O NE cannot find anything more religious and more joyful in sacred celebrations than a whole congregation expressing its faith and devotion in song. Therefore the active participation of the whole people, which is shown in singing, is to be carefully promoted.

Constitution on the
Sacred Liturgy

T HE priests came out of the holy place (for all the priests who were present had sanctified themselves, without regard to their divisions, and all the levitical singers, Asaph, Heman, and Jeduthun, their sons and kindred, arrayed in fine linen, with cymbals, harps and lyres, stood east of the altar with 120 priests who were trumpeters). It was the duty of the trumpeters and singers to make themselves heard in unison in praise and thanksgiving to the LORD, and when the song was raised, with trumpets and cymbals and other musical instruments, in praise to the LORD,

"For he is good,
for his steadfast love endures forever,"

the house, the house of the LORD, was filled with a cloud, so that the priests could not stand to minister because of the cloud; for the glory of the LORD filled the house of God.

2 Chronicles 5:11–14

Robert Browning
Nineteenth century

W HO hears music, feels his solitude peopled at once.

THEREFORE it is fitting for you to run your race together with the bishop's purpose — as you do. For your presbytery — worthy of fame, worthy of God — is attuned to the bishop like strings to a lyre. Therefore by your unity and harmonious love Jesus Christ is sung. Each of you must be part of this chorus so that, being harmonious in unity, receiving God's pitch in unison, you may sing with one voice through Jesus Christ to the Father, so that he may both hear you and recognize you, through what you do well, as members of his Son. Therefore it is profitable for you to be in blameless unison, so that you may always participate in God.

Ignatius of Antioch
First century

HEAVEN's not a place
Where time doth race
Across the flatted fields of edgeless space
Thou shalt not hear its news, nor its retreat discover.
No! 'tis a dance
Where love perpetual,
Rhythmical,
Musical,
Maketh advance
Loved one to lover.

Evelyn Underhill

JOYFUL, joyful, we adore you,
God of glory,
Lord of love;
Hearts unfold like flowers before you,
Opening to the sun above.
Melt the clouds of sin and sadness;
Drive the dark of doubt away;
Giver of immortal gladness,
Fill us with the light of day!

All your works with joy surround you,
Earth and heav'n reflect your rays,
Stars and angels sing around you,
Center of unbroken praise;
Field and forest, vale and mountain,
Flowery meadow, flashing sea,
Chanting bird and flowing fountain,
Praising you eternally!

Always giving and forgiving,
Ever blessing, ever blest,
Wellspring of the joy of living,
Ocean depth of happy rest!
Loving Father,
Christ our brother,
Let your light upon us shine;
Teach us how to love each other,
Lift us to the joy divine.

Mortals join the mighty chorus,
Which the morning stars began;
God's own love is reigning o'er us,
Joining people hand in hand.
Ever singing, march we onward,
Victors in the midst of strife;
Joyful music leads us sunward
In the triumph song of life.

Henry van Dyke

Music is sweet from the thrush's throat!
 Oh little thrush
 With the holy note,
Like a footstep of God in a sick-room's hush
 My soul you crush.

Unstopped organ, from earth you break
 To knock at the skies,
 And I can but shake
My fragile fetters, and with you rise
 Into Paradise.

But Love, your music requires not wings.
 To the common breed
 It clings, and sings:
"Heaven on earth is Heaven indeed.
 This is my creed."

E. E. Cummings

HE who finds himself gifted with a tunable Voice, and yet neglects to cultivate it, not only hides in the Earth a Talent of the highest value, but robs himself of that peculiar Pleasure, of which they only are conscious who exercise that Faculty.

William Billings
Eighteenth century

NO sunset, but a grey, great, struggling sky
Full of strong silence. In green cloisters throng
Shy nuns of evening, telling beads of song.
Swallows, like winged prayers, soar steadily by,
Hallowing twilight. From the faint and high,
Night waves her misting censers, and along
The world, the singing rises into strong,
Pure peace. Now earth and heaven twain raptures die.

I knew your presence in the twilight mist,
In the world-filling darkness, in the rain
That spoke in whispers, — for the world was kissed
And laid in sleep. — These wild, sweet, perfect things
Are little miracles your memory sings,
Till heart on heart makes us one music again.

E. E. Cummings

I think people who can truly live a life in music are telling the world, "You can have my love, you can have my smiles. Forget the bad parts, you don't need them. Just take the music, the goodness, because it's the very best and it's the part I give most willingly."

George Harrison

AH, Lord, the torment of this task that Thou hast laid
   on me
To tell the splendour of Thy love!

I sing, and sing,
Yet all the while the truth evadeth telling:

No words there are, no words,
To show Thee as Thou art:

These songs of mine are chaff,
No spark of living truth hath ever lit my lips:

Ah, Lord, the torment of this task that Thou hast laid on me!   Tukaram

ALL creatures of our God and King,
Lift up your voice and with us sing:
  Alleluia! Alleluia!
O burning sun with golden beam
And silver moon with softer gleam:
  Alleluia! Alleluia!
  Alleluia, alleluia, alleluia!

O rushing wind and breezes soft,
O clouds that ride the winds aloft:
  Alleluia! Alleluia!
O rising morn, in praise rejoice,
O lights of evening, find a voice.
  Alleluia! Alleluia!
  Alleluia, alleluia, alleluia!

O flowing waters, pure and clear,
Make music for your Lord to hear.
  Alleluia! Alleluia!
O fire so masterful and bright,
Providing us with warmth and light,
  Alleluia! Alleluia!
  Alleluia, alleluia, alleluia!

Dear mother earth, who day by day
Unfolds rich blessings on our way,
  Alleluia! Alleluia!
The fruits and flow'rs that verdant grow,
Let them God's glory also show.
  Alleluia! Alleluia!
  Alleluia, alleluia, alleluia!

O every one of tender heart,
Forgiving others, take your part,
    Alleluia! Alleluia!
All you who pain and sorrow bear,
Praise God and cast on God your care.
    Alleluia! Alleluia!
    Alleluia, alleluia, alleluia!

And you, most kind and gentle death,
Waiting to hush our final breath,
    Alleluia! Alleluia!
You lead to heav'n the child of God,
Where Christ our Lord the way has trod.
    Alleluia! Alleluia!
    Alleluia, alleluia, alleluia!

Let all things their Creator bless,
And worship God in humbleness,
    Alleluia! Alleluia!
Oh praise the Father, praise the Son,
And praise the Spirit, Three in One!
    Alleluia! Alleluia!
    Alleluia, alleluia, alleluia!

Francis of Assisi
Thirteenth century

Praise the Lord!
  Across the heavens,
from the heights,
all you angels, heavenly beings,
sing praise, sing praise!

Sun and moon, glittering stars,
sing praise, sing praise.
Highest heavens, rain clouds,
sing praise, sing praise.

Praise God's name,
whose word called you forth
and fixed you in place for ever
by eternal decree.

Let there be praise:
from depths of the earth,
from creatures of the deep.

Fire and hail, snow and mist,
storms, winds,
mountains, hills,
fruit trees and cedars,
wild beasts and tame,
snakes and birds,

princes, judges,
rulers, subjects,
men, women,
old and young,
praise, praise the holy name,
this name beyond all names.

God's splendor above the earth,
above the heavens,
gives strength to the nation,
glory to the faithful,
a people close to the Lord.
Psalm 148   Israel, let there be praise!

As I came to the edge of the woods,
Thrush music — hark!
Now if it was dusk outside,
Inside it was dark.

Too dark in the woods for a bird
By sleight of wing
To better its perch for the night,
Though it still could sing.

The last of the light of the sun
That had died in the west
Still lived for one song more
In a thrush's breast.

Far in the pillared dark
Thrush music went —
Almost like a call to come in
To the dark and lament.

But no, I was out for stars:
I would not come in.
I meant not even if asked,
And I hadn't been.

Robert Frost

Once in an Abbey-church, the while we prayed
 All silent at the lifting of the Host,
A little bird through some high window strayed;
     And to and fro
     Like a wee angel lost
That on a sudden finds its heaven below,
     It went the morning long,
And made our Eucharist more glad with song.

It sang, it sang! and as the quiet priest
     Far off about the lighted altar moved
The awful substance of that mystic feast
     All hushed before,
     It, like a thing that loved
Yet loved in liberty, would plunge and soar
     Beneath the vault in play
And thence toss down the oblation of its lay.

The walls that went our sanctuary around
     Did, as of old, to that sweet summons yield.
New scents and sounds within our gates were found;
     The cry of kine,
     The fragrance of the field,
All woodland whispers, hastened to the shrine:
     The country-side was come
Eager and joyful, to its spirit's home.

Far-stretched I saw the cornfield and the plough,
   The scudding cloud, the cleanly-running brook,
The humble, kindly turf, the tossing bough
      That all their light
     From Love's own furnace took—
This altar, where one angel brownly bright
     Proclaimed the sylvan creed,
And sang the Benedictus of the mead.

All earth was lifted to communion then,
   All lovely life was there to meet its King;
Ah, not the little arid souls of men
      But sun and wind
     And all desirous thing
The ground of their beseeching here did find;
   All with one self-same bread,
And all by one eternal priest, were fed.
                              Evelyn Underhill

WE probably derive all our basic rhythms and themes from Nature, which offers them to us, pregnant with meaning, in every animal noise.
                              Gustav Mahler

I shall take the most banal example: that of the pleasure we experience on hearing the murmur of the breeze in the trees, the rippling of a brook, the song of a bird. All this pleases us, diverts us, delights us. We may even say: "What lovely music!" Naturally, we are speaking only in terms of comparison. But then, *comparison* is not *reason*. These natural sounds suggest music to us, but are not yet themselves music. If we take pleasure in these sounds by imagining that on being exposed to them we become musicians and even, momentarily, creative musicians, we must admit that we are fooling ourselves. They are promises of music; it takes a human being to keep them: a human being who is sensitive to nature's many voices, of course, but who in addition feels the need of putting them in order and who is gifted for that task with a very special aptitude. In his hands all that I have considered as not being music will become music.

Igor Stravinsky

You tend and water the land.
    How wonderful the harvest!
You fill your springs,
    ready the seeds, prepare the grain.

You soak the furrows
and level the ridges.
With softening rain
you bless the land with growth.

You crown the year with riches.
All you touch comes alive:
untilled lands yield crops,
hills are dressed in joy,

flocks clothe the pastures,
valleys wrap themselves in grain.
They all shout for joy
and break into song.

Psalm 65:10–14

Dear God,
I don't know how to pray by myself
very well,
but will You please
protect my little nest from wind and rain?
Put a great deal of dew on the flowers,
many seeds in my way.
Make Your blue very high,
Your branches lissom;
let Your kind light stay late in the sky
and set my heart brimming with such music
that I must sing, sing, sing. . . .
Please, Lord.

Amen

Carmen Bernos de
Gasztold

We cannot doubt that animals both love and practice music. That is evident. But it seems their musical system differs from ours. It is another school. . . . We are not familiar with their didactic works. Perhaps they don't have any.

Erik Satie

Let angels and archangels,
Dominions, thrones, and pow'rs,
With cherubim and seraphs
Now join in joyful choirs.
Sing glory in the highest
And peace in earth and heav'n.
Oh, tell the words of wonder,
"Fear not! Good news is giv'n."

To startled, sleepy shepherds
Out with their flocks at night
Appear the hosts of heaven
With glee and great delight.
"To you in David's city
A Savior has been born.
As joy to troubled spirits
And hope to hearts forlorn."

Those hushed resplendent voices,
Those silent rustling wings,
Those swift and patient watchers
Surround our snuggling king.
Angelic alleluias
As earth has never known
Change barn to tabernacle
And manger into throne.

The angels who sing glory
will one day wait in pain
As mortals crucify him—
Yet seal the stone in vain;
For angels on the third day
Proclaim the empty tomb,
"The firstborn of creation
Has burst death's ancient womb."

Sylvia Dunstan

THE Cherubim and six-winged Seraphim, their feet covered with two, their heads with two, and flying with two, saying together with thousand times thousands of archangels and ten-thousand times ten-thousands of angels, without ceasing and in a loud voice; and let all the people say with them, "Holy, holy, holy, Lord of Sabaoth, heaven and earth are full of his glory: blessed be he for ever; Amen."

Apostolic Constitutions

THE Recording Angel I am concerned with is not CBS, in any case, but the One with the Big Book.

Igor Stravinsky

WHERE the bright seraphim in burning row
Their loud up-lifted Angel trumpets blow.

John Milton
Seventeenth century

THE angels all were singing out of tune,
And hoarse with having little else to do.

Lord Byron
Nineteenth century

WHEN he had taken the scroll, the four living creatures and the twenty-four elders fell before the Lamb, each holding a harp and golden bowls full of incense, which are the prayers of the saints. They sing a new song:

"You are worthy to take the scroll
   and to open its seals,
for you were slaughtered and by your blood you
      ransomed for God
   saints from every tribe and language and people
      and nation;
you have made them to be a kingdom and priests
      serving our God,
and they will reign on earth."

Then I looked, and I heard the voice of many angels surrounding the throne and the living creatures and the elders; they numbered myriads of myriads and thousands of thousands, singing with full voice,

"Worthy is the Lamb that was slaughtered
to receive power and wealth and wisdom and might
and honor and glory and blessing!"

Then I heard every creature in heaven and on earth and under the earth and in the sea, and all that is in them, singing,

"To the one seated on the throne and to the Lamb
be blessing and honor and glory and might
forever and ever!"

And the four living creatures said, "Amen!" And the elders fell down and worshiped.

Revelation 5:8–14

To play the organ properly one should have a vision of Eternity.

Charles-Marie Widor

THE Apocalypse also shows us those who have gone through the sea, that is, who have triumphed over death, singing the Canticle of Moses and the song of the Lamb (15:2 – 4). . . . As Dom Winzen says, the canticle of Miriam was "the hour in which the Divine Office was born." The singing of hymns in the Christian community fulfills the figure of the canticle of the Exodus and prefigures the heavenly liturgy.

Jean Danielou

FOR in Christ's coach saints sweetly sing As they to glory ride therein.

Edward Taylor
Eighteenth century

Praise ought to be given to the heavenly creator with the unceasing voice of heart and mouth. For the creator gives grace not only to those standing and erect, but also to those sliding and falling out of their very high seats.

Thereupon, you see, O people, the sky got very bright. This stands for the joy of the heavenly city. And I heard all the previously mentioned virtues sing in a wondrous manner to the various types of music. They persisted strongly in the way of truth as they sang the praises of the city of celestial joy. They persisted strongly as they called those with complaints back to praising with joy. This signifies that you hear a pleasant and sweet musical performance sounding forth from the chosen ones with wondrous joy as they sing about all the wonderful things of God which have been prophesied to you. This is just like the air containing and sustaining all those things which are under heaven. This musical performance exists in the heavenly city and perseveres in God with pleasant devotion. It also exists in the complaints of those whom the old serpent has tried to destroy, but whom divine virtue nevertheless has led through to the company of blessed joy. The blessed joy contains those mysteries which the human mind cannot know while on earth.

Hildegard of Bingen
Twelfth century

A ND I saw what appeared to be a sea of glass mixed with fire, and those who had conquered the beast and its image and the number of its name, standing beside the sea of glass with harps of God in their hands. And they sing the song of Moses, the servant of God, and the song of the Lamb:

"Great and amazing are your deeds,
    Lord God the Almighty!
Just and true are your ways,
    King of the nations!
Lord, who will not fear
    and glorify your name?
For you alone are holy.
    All nations will come
    and worship before you,
for your judgments have been revealed."

Revelation 15:2–4

A ND the sound was that of the voice of a multitude singing a musical performance with harmony in praise of the celestial orders. This is because the musical performance recalls the glory and honor of the heavenly city. And it bears glory and honor upwards again since it brings forth the word of God publicly.

Hildegard of Bingen
Twelfth century

SINCE I am coming to that holy room,
Where, with the choir of saints forevermore,
I shall be made thy music: as I come
I tune the instrument here at the door,
And what I must do then, think here before.

John Donne
Seventeenth century

THEN, crowned again, their golden harps they took,
Harps ever tuned, that glittering by their side
Like quivers hung; and with preamble sweet
Of charming symphony they introduce
Their sacred song, and waken raptures high;
No voice exempt, no voice but well could join
Melodious part; such concord is in heaven.

John Milton
Seventeenth century

JERUSALEM, my happy home,
When shall I with you be?
When shall my sorrows have an end?
Your joys when shall I see?

Your saints are crowned with glory great;
They see God face to face;
They triumph still, they still rejoice:
In that most holy place.

There David stands with harp in hand
As master of the choir:
Ten thousand times that we were blest
That might this music hear.

Our Lady sings Magnificat
With tune surpassing sweet;
And all the virgins join the song
While sitting at her feet.

There Magdalene has left her tears,
And cheerfully does sing
With blessed saints, whose harmony
In ev'ry street does ring.

Jerusalem, Jerusalem,
God grant that I may see
Your endless joy, and of the same
Partaker ever be!

Joseph Bromehead
Nineteenth century

THE air of Paradise
   is a fountain of delight
from which Adam sucked
   when he was young;
its very breath, like a mother's breast,
   gave him nourishment in his childhood.
He was young, fair,
   and full of joy,
but when he spurned the injunction
   he grew old, sad and decrepit;
he bore old age
   as a burden of woes.

No harmful frost,
   no scorching heat
is to be found
   in that blessed place of delight;
it is a harbor of joys,
   a haven of pleasures;
light and rejoicing
   have their home there;
gathered there are to be found
   harps and lyres,
with shouts of Hosanna,
   and the Church crying, "Alleluia."

Ephrem
Fourth century

MUSICIANS wrestle everywhere—
All day—among the crowded air
I hear the silver strife—
And—waking—long before the morn—
Such transport breaks upon the town
I think it that "New Life"!

It is not Bird—it has no nest—
Nor "Band"—in brass and scarlet—drest—
Nor Tamborin—nor Man—
It is not Hymn from pulpit read—
The "Morning Stars" the Treble led
On Time's first Afternoon!

Some—say—it is "the Spheres"—at play!
Some say that bright Majority
Of vanished Dames—and Men!
Some—think it service in the place
Where we—with late—celestial face—
Please God—shall Ascertain!

Emily Dickinson
Nineteenth century

CHARLEMAGNE too was struck, when in Rome, by the discordance between Roman and Gallican singing; while the Franks argued that their chant was corrupted by our chanters with some poor melodies, ours probably showed the authentic antiphonal. On that occasion, so the story goes, Charlemagne asked whether the stream or the source carried the clearer water. When they answered the source, he added wisely, "Then we too, who till now drank the troubled water from the stream, must go back to the clarity of the source." Hence he soon left two of his assiduous clerics with Hadrian. After good instruction they restored for him the early chant at Metz and, by way of Metz, all over Gaul.

John the Deacon
Ninth century

So far as can be seen, if the seventh and eighth centuries were the golden age of Roman music, the ninth and tenth saw the finest compositions of the monastic precentors. There resulted a corpus of church music which has never been surpassed in gravity, variety and flexibility for the voices of boys and men. With their variety of solo, antiphon and chorus they gave perhaps the highest aesthetic satisfaction enjoyed by any in that age. It was noted that the stone barrel-vault was particularly resonant for the voices of a large choir.

David Knowles with
Dimitri Obolensky

THE challenge is to look deeply enough to discover that this darkness is all that we need, and to find in it what we are looking for. Listening deeply to chant, we will hear a darkness turned into sound, a darkness that shines.

At Terce we pray that this fire of the Holy Spirit, this life-breath of the Holy Spirit, may set our heart aflame. We pray that this fire may also be spread in the world in the sense of Jesus' words, "I've come to cast fire on the world, and how I wish that it may blaze." It is the time to spread the fiery enthusiasm of the divine life within us throughout the worlds we live in.

It is easy to cast a jaundiced eye at happily pious people who are always saying "Thanks be to God" and "God be willing" and "Blessed be" this and that. But they often can have a simple but intense sense that life is a gift, and that they are part of a divinely charged world. Many of us know that it is the simple faithful — and not the sophisticated — who have the deepest spirituality.

Our feeling of being ill at ease in the world, which I spoke of earlier, signals our longing to share in that flow of blessing, to experience God's spirit in true enthusiasm, to feel that *joie de vivre* that is not just a passing mood. Chant is the music that expresses our connection to the whole. It tells us that ultimately, we are not orphaned, we are not alienated. We have the spirit of the universe flowing through our body. It flows as song out our mouths.

David Steindl-Rast

THE chastening of church music would produce some surprising consequences in the next centuries. While Gregory's aim was not aesthetic, the chanted liturgy offered fantastic opportunities for creation and variation. These would be richly explored in the Mass, the sacred daily reenactment of the Last Supper, and in the Divine Office, which consisted of eight daily prayer services for assigned hours of the day. Every day of the ecclesiastical year acquired its own Mass and Office, which varied according to two cycles, one celebrating the fixed feasts (Proper of the Saints) and another celebrating the movable feasts (Proper of the Time).

We would make a great mistake, then, to think of the Gregorian chant (plainsong or plainchant) as monotonous or simply repetitive. More than eleven thousand tunes or texts of medieval chants survive in manuscript form, "graduals" for the Mass, and antiphonaries for the Office, along with notated missals and breviaries. While the Gregorian chants are monophonic music with a single melodic line, their words invited countless variations. Parts of the liturgy became chants in which each syllable was pronounced to a single musical note. Others became "neumatic" chants, with clusters of notes in series, sometimes as many as a dozen accompanying a single syllable. And then the subtly florid "melismatic" chants would set a single vowel to two hundred or more notes.

It is conceivable that the Iconoclasts might have won against music as they nearly had against images a millennium before. The Council of Trent (1545–63), doing the work of the Catholic Counter-Reformation, might have inhibited church music by draconian measures, but finally went no further than to condemn everything "impure or lascivious" to preserve the House of God as the House of Prayer.

The Council of Trent reflected the ongoing battle between the music of the word and the music of instruments. The main objection to polyphony had been its disregard for sacred words, and the council finally decreed that future church music must be more simply written so the words could be clearly understood.

Daniel J. Boorstin

WITH the understanding that unity and harmony stood in opposition to duality and disharmony the primitive church rejected all heterophony and polyphony. The greatest possible harmony was pursued as the musical expression of the union of souls and of the community, as it prevails in the early Christian liturgy. It is in this sense that the entire community of Christians, according to Clement of Alexandria, becomes a single symphonia:

"We want to strive so that we, the many, may be brought together into one love, according to the union of the essential unity. As we do good may we similarly pursue unity. . . . The union of many, which the divine harmony has called forth out of a medley of sounds and division, becomes one symphony, following the one leader of the choir and teacher, the Word, resting in the same truth and crying out: 'Abba, Father. . . .'"

The ideal of early Christian singing was unity or monophony. The most ancient evidence for this is probably found in the prefaces of the Mass, which speak of the angels and archangels, cherubim and seraphim, *qui non cessant clamare quotidie una voce dicentes: Sanctus, Sanctus, Sanctus Dominus Deus Sabaoth.*

Johannes Quasten

How all's to one thing wrought!
The members, how they sit!
O what a tune the thought
Must be that fancied it.

Nor angel insight can
Learn how the heart is hence:
Since all the make of man
Is law's indifference.

[Who shaped these walls has shewn
The music of his mind,
Made known, though thick through stone
What beauty beat behind.]

Not free in this because
His powers seemed free to play:
He swept what scope he was
To sweep and must obey.

Though down his being's bent
Like air he changed in choice,
That was an instrument
Which overvaulted voice.

What makes the man and what
The man within that makes:
Ask whom he serves or not
Serves and what side he takes.

For good grows wild and wide,
Has shades, is nowhere none;
But right must seek a side
And choose for chieftain one.

Therefore this masterhood,
This piece of perfect song,
This fault-not-found-with good
Is neither right nor wrong,

No more than red or blue,
No more than Re and Mi,
Or sweet the golden glue
That's built for by the bee.

[Who built these walls made known
The music of his mind,
Yet here he has but shewn
His ruder-rounded rind.
His brightest blooms lie there unblown,
His sweetest nectar hides behind.]

Gerard Manley
Hopkins
Nineteenth century

THE power of music is so great and at the same time so direct that people tend to think of it in a static fashion, as if it had always been what we today know it to be. It is scarcely possible to realize how extraordinary the march of Western music has been without considering briefly its historical origins. Musicologists tell us that the music of the early Christian church was monodic — that is, it was music of a single melodic line. Its finest flower was Gregorian chant. But think what daring it took for composers to attempt the writing of music in more than a single part. This novel conception began to impose itself about a thousand years ago, yet the marvel of it is still a cause for wonder.

Aaron Copland

THERE is no real creating without hard work. That which you would call invention — that is to say, a thought, an idea — is simply an inspiration for which I am not responsible, which is no merit of mine. It is a present, a gift, which I ought even to despise until I have made it my own by dint of hard work.

Johannes Brahms
Nineteenth century

MAGIC is what we do. Music is the way we do it.

Jerry Garcia

FOR the glory of the most high God alone,
And for my neighbour to learn from.

Johann Sebastian Bach
Eighteenth century

JUDITH began this thanksgiving before all Israel, and all the people loudly sang this song of praise. And Judith said,

Begin a song to my God with tambourines,
   sing to my LORD with cymbals.
Raise to him a new psalm;
   exalt him, and call upon his name.
For the LORD is a God who crushes wars;
   he sets up his camp among his people;
   he delivered me from the hands of my pursuers.

Judith 15:14; 16:1–2

I get up early, and as soon as I have dressed I go down on my knees and pray God and the Blessed Virgin that I may have another successful day. Then when I've had some breakfast I sit down at the clavier and begin my search. If I hit on an idea quickly, it goes ahead easily and without much trouble. But if I can't get on, I know that I must have forfeited God's grace by some fault of mine, and then I pray once more for grace till I feel I'm forgiven.

Joseph Haydn
Eighteenth century

I haven't thought about it in some kind of methodical "now I'm gonna make music that makes people dance" way, but just in terms of "Why do these things work? Why do some things work and some things not work?"

Jerry Garcia

WE must not suppose that composers invent their music out of the blue, without forerunners or surroundings. The innovators are the small men who set the ball rolling. The big men come at the end of a period and sum it up. Thus it was with Bach. The period of Haydn and Mozart, not to speak of the smaller people like Cherubini and Hummel, led the way to the supreme master, Beethoven. We can trace the art of Wagner through the early *Singspiele* of Adam Hiller and his contemporaries in the eighteenth century, through Weber and Marschner, to find its culmination in *Die Meistersinger* and *Tristan*. These were the right men coming at the right time and under the right circumstances; that is what enabled them to be great. Sometimes the potentially right man comes at the wrong time. Purcell, for example, was a bit too early for his flower to bloom fully; Sullivan, who in other circumstances might have written a *Figaro,* was thwarted by mid-Victorian inhibitions: the public thought that great music must be portentous and solemn, an oratorio, or a sacred cantata at the least, and that comic opera was beneath notice as a work of art.

R. Vaughn Williams

COMPOSERS do not often hear the music that is being played; it only serves as an impulse for something quite different — for the creation of music that only lives in their imagination. It is a sort of schizophrenia — we are listening to something and at the same time creating something else.

Witold Lutostawski

Not from me—
it came from above.

Joseph Haydn
Eighteenth century

ALTHOUGH there are many musical instruments, the prophet made this book suited to the psaltery, as it is called, revealing, it seems to me, the grace from on high which sounded in him through the Holy Spirit, since this alone, of all musical instruments, has the source of its sound above. For the brass wires of the cithara and the lyre sound from below against the plectrum, but the psaltery has the origins of its harmonious rhythms above, in order that we may study to seek for those things which are on high and not be drawn down by the pleasantness of the melody to the passions of the flesh. And I think that by reason of this structure of the instrument the words of the prophet profoundly and wisely reveal to us that those whose souls are attuned and harmonious have an easy path to things above.

Basil
Fourth century

I am the strings, and the Supreme is the musician.

Carlos Santana

IF your talent is choir or organ, there's no problem. Choir members and organists can be sure their gift is from God because who else but God would be interested. Just like nobody gets fat on celery, nobody goes into church music for the wrong motives.

Garrison Keillor

Rise, heart; thy Lord is risen. Sing his praise
    Without delays,
Who takes thee by the hand, that thou likewise
    With him may'st rise:
That, as his death calcined thee to dust,
His life may make thee gold, and much more, Just.

Awake, my lute, and struggle for thy part
    With all thy art.
The cross taught all wood to resound his name
    Who bore the same.
His stretched sinews taught all strings, what key
Is best to celebrate this most high day.

Consort both heart and lute, and twist a song
    Pleasant and long:
Or since all music is but three parts vied,
    And multiplied:
O let thy blessed Spirit bear a part,
And make up our defects with his sweet art.

George Herbert
Seventeenth century

Our priests, I ask of you:
From whence come the flowers that enrapture man?
The songs that intoxicate, the lovely songs?

Only from His home do they come, from the innermost
        part of heaven,
only from there comes the myriad of flowers. . . .
Where the nectar of the flowers is found
the fragrant beauty of the flower is refined. . . .
They interlace, they interweave;
among them sings, among them warbles the quetzal bird.

The flowers sprout, they are fresh, they grow;
they open their blossoms,
and from within emerge the flowers of song;
among men You scatter them, You send them.
You are the singer!

Nahuatl sage

You should understand this from the case of the harp
or lyre or cymbals when they make a sound: does the
sweetness of the melody and song come from the harp or
the lyre, or does it belong to the person plucking the instrument and singing? You, who are endowed with reason,
should receive instruction from what is not endowed with
senses, and you should realize that the Spirit of God is playing on your tongue, and singing his melodies in your mouth.

Martyrius
Seventh century

Oblack and unknown bards of long ago,
   How came your lips to touch the sacred fire?
How, in your darkness, did you come to know
The power and beauty of the minstrel's lyre?
Who first from midst his bonds lifted his eyes?
Who first from out the still watch, lone and long,
Feeling the ancient faith of prophets rise
Within his dark-kept soul, burst into song?

Heart of what slave poured out such melody
As "Steal Away to Jesus"? On its strains
His spirit must have nightly floated free,
Though still about his hands he felt his chains.
Who heard great "Jordan roll"? Whose starward eye
Saw chariot "swing low"? And who was he
That breathed that comforting, melodic sigh,
"Nobody knows de trouble I see"?

What merely living clod, what captive thing,
Could up toward God through all its darkness grope,
And find within its deadened heart to sing
These songs of sorrow, love and faith, and hope?
How did it catch that subtle undertone,
That note in music heard not with the ears?
How sound the elusive reed so seldom blown,
Which stirs the soul or melts the heart to tears?

Not that great German master in his dream
Of harmonies that thundered amongst the stars
At the creation, ever heard a theme
Nobler than "Go down, Moses." Mark its bars,
How like a mighty trumpet call they stir
The blood. Such are the notes that men have sung
Going to valorous deeds; such tones there were
That helped make history when time was young.

There is a wide, wide wonder in it all,
That from degraded rest and servile toil
The fiery spirit of the seer should call
These simple children of the sun and soil.
O black slave singers, gone forgot, unfamed,
You — you alone, of all the long, long line
Of those who've sung untaught, unknown, unnamed,
Have stretched out upward, seeking the divine.
You sang not deeds of heroes or of kings;

No chant of bloody wars, no exulting paean
Of arms-won triumphs; but your humble strings
You touched in chord with music empyrean.
You sang far better than you knew; the songs
That for your listeners' hungry hearts sufficed
Still live, — but more than this to you belongs:
You sang a race from wood and stone to Christ.   James Weldon Johnson

Do nothing from selfish ambition or conceit, but in humility regard others as better than yourselves. Let each of you look not to your own interests, but to the interests of others. Let the same mind be in you that was in Christ Jesus, who, though he was in the form of God, did not regard equality with God as something to be exploited, but emptied himself, taking the form of a slave, being born in human likeness. And being found in human form, he humbled himself and became obedient to the point of death — even death on a cross. Therefore God also highly exalted him and gave him the name that is above every name, so that at the name of Jesus every knee should bend, in heaven and on earth and under the earth, and every tongue should confess that Jesus Christ is Lord, to the glory of God the Father.

Therefore, my beloved, just as you have always obeyed me, not only in my presence, but much more now in my absence, work out your own salvation with fear and trembling; for it is God who is at work in you, enabling you both to will and to work for his good pleasure.

Philippians 2:3–13

Blessed be you, O God,
who gave the birds their song,
the whales their hum,
the lions their roar,
and the ocean waves their beat.

Blessed be you for tuning the soul
to the rhythms and songs of praise
that fill your creation.

Blessed be you for poets and prophets
who have honored your word
in ecstatic speech
and faithful proclamation.

Blessed be you
for composers, singers and instrumentalists
who have attended to your Spirit,
drawing music
from the silent hallelujahs of the heart,
shaping breath and sound
to the glory of your name.

Blessed be you for congregations
who have filled their lives with faith
and their voices with song.

Blessed be you for every creature
who joins to proclaim:
How great is your name in all the earth!

Thomas H. Troeger

WHEN the morning stars together
Their Creator's glory sang,
And the angel host all shouted
Till with joy the heavens rang,
Then Your wisdom and Your greatness
Their exultant music told,
All the beauty and the splendor
Which Your mighty works unfold.

When in synagogue and temple
Voices raised the psalmists' songs,
Offering the adoration
Which alone to You belongs,
When the singers and the cymbals
With the trumpet made accord,
Glory filled the house of worship,
And all knew Your presence, Lord.

Voice and instrument in union
Through the ages spoke Your praise,
Plain-song, tuneful hymns, and anthems
Told Your faithful, gracious ways.
Choir and orchestra and organ
Each a sacred offering brought,
While, inspired by Your own Spirit,
Poet and composer wrought.

Lord, we bring our gift of music;
Touch our lips and fire our hearts,
Teach our minds and train our senses,
Fit us for these sacred arts.
Then with skill and consecration
We would serve You, Lord, and give
All our powers to glorify You,
Albert F. Bayly   And in serving fully live.

Lord, how diverse and splendid are the melodies
    we sing.
Each song is unique to itself,
    like nothing heard before.
What a wonder it is that men and women continue
    to create new, unheard music.
Like snowflakes and thumbprints that are never alike,
Creation continues in human works.
The Creator joins with the Spirit to sing a
    new unending song through the channels of humankind.
Each composer brings forth something unsaid,
Something ears have never heard for all time,
And God is magnified in their efforts.
How beautifully, wonderfully made are we!
So privileged to be made in the image and likeness of God.
A creator who delights in our song.
Who anticipates with us each new work.
We praise you, Creator-Spirit, for such unending beauty
    stemming forth from the seed gift you have planted in us.   Jeanne Hunt

YOUR voices tune, and raise them high,
Till they echo from the vaulted sky
the blest Cecilia's name.

Music to heav'n and her we owe,
The greatest blessing that's below;
Sound loudly then her fame!

Let's imitate her notes above,
And may this evening ever prove
Sacred to harmony, sacred to love.

Newburgh Hamilton

IN a garden shady this holy lady
With reverent cadence and subtle psalm,
Like a black swan as death came on
Poured forth her song in perfect calm:
And by ocean's margin this innocent virgin
Constructed an organ to enlarge her prayer,
And notes tremendous from her great engine
Thundered out on the Roman air.

Blonde Aphrodite rose up excited,
Moved to delight by the melody,
White as an orchid she rode quite naked
In an oyster shell on top of the sea;
At sounds so entrancing the angels dancing
Came out of their trance into time again,
And around the wicked in Hell's abysses
The huge flame flickered and eased their pain.

Blessed Cecilia, appear in visions
To all musicians, appear and inspire:
Translated Daughter, come down and startle
Composing mortals with immortal fire.

W. H. Auden

WHILE the clock was striking five, he carried the completed manuscript across a corner of the quadrangle to the small concert-chamber where composition was usually taught. The ceiling and four wall-panels had been painted with scenes from the life of St. Cecilia, including what was now known to be her unhistorical martyrdom in the year 230. The artist was supposed to have been a mid-eighteenth-century Prefect of Music at the Chapel, and although it was also supposed, or at least hoped, that he had been a better musician than artist, most folk enjoyed what he had painted. Hubert did; as he mounted the low platform and sat down at one of the two piano-fortes there, he gave the figure of the saint's husband, known to generations of clerks as "the tipsy Roman," an affectionate glance. Raising the lid of the instrument, he began to play the Prometheus Variations, Beethoven's last complete keyboard work. It would never do to be caught tinkling some trash of one's own.

Kingsley Amis

WITH singing instruments, Cecilia cried to the Lord, saying: Let my heart be pure, that I not be defiled.

Liber Usualis

Fʀᴏᴍ harmony, from heavenly harmony
     This universal frame began:
   When Nature underneath a heap
      Of jarring atoms lay,
    And could not heave her head,
The tuneful voice was heard from high:
     "Arise, ye more than dead."
Then cold, and hot, and moist, and dry,
In order to their stations leap,
   And Music's power obey.
From harmony, from heavenly harmony
      This universal frame began:
    From harmony to harmony
Through all the compass of the notes it ran,
The diapason closing full in man.

What passion cannot Music raise and quell!
     When Jubal struck the corded shell,
   His listening brethren stood around,
   And, wondering, on their faces fell
   To worship that celestial sound.
Less than a god they thought there could not dwell
   Within the hollow of that shell
   That spoke so sweetly and so well.
What passion cannot Music raise and quell!

Orpheus could lead the savage race;
And trees unrooted left their place,
   Sequacious of the lyre;
But bright Cecilia raised the wonder higher:
When to her organ vocal breath was given,
An angel heard, and straight appeared,
   Mistaking earth for heaven.

As from the power of sacred lays
   The spheres began to move,
And sung the great Creator's praise
   To all the blest above;
So, when the last and dreadful hour
This crumbling pageant shall devour,
The trumpet shall be heard on high,
The dead shall live, the living die,
And Music shall untune the sky.

John Dryden
Seventeenth century

IN 1584 the newly founded Academy of Music in Rome chose Cecilia as its patron saint. St. Cecilia's Day (22 November) became a yearly festival of music. Her patronage may derive from a misunderstanding of the word *organum,* Latin for "musical instrument," in the *Acts* of her martyrdom, in which it was said that at her wedding feast "as the musical instruments were sounding, she sang in her heart to the Lord," praying that she might remain unsullied. This gave rise to the legend that she invented the organ, which she is shown playing.

J.C.J. Metford

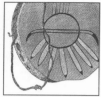

John Ayto

ETYMOLOGICALLY, *music* comes from the "muses," Greek goddesses who inspired poets, painters, musicians, etc. The word traces its history back via Old French *musique* and Latin *musica* to Greek *mousiké*, a noun use of *mousikós* "of the muses," an adjective derived from *mousa* "muse." The specialization of the word's meaning began in Greek—first to "poetry sung to music," and subsequently to "music" alone.

Gustave Flaubert
Nineteenth century

HUMAN speech is like a cracked kettle on which we tap crude rhythms for bears to dance to, while we long to make music that will melt the stars.

Paul Valéry

WORDS are adapted to great rhythms. . . . Great rhythms absorb words.

I N the tradition of the synagogue, the reading of the sacred text was hardly ever done without chanting. It was taught that the one who reads Scripture without chanting is guilty of idolatry.

A similar chanting of sacred texts is found in numerous religious traditions, most especially in the Islamic tradition that traces chanting of the Koran back to the prophet himself. It may be explained by the desire to tear the sacred word from the banality of a profane reading and to amplify its inherent worth by the magic of melody and rhythm.

Lucien Deiss

L ET the word be master of the melody, not its slave.

Claudio Monteverdi
Seventeenth century

M USIC is the exaltation of poetry. Both of them may excel apart, but surely they are most excellent when they are joined, because nothing is then wanting to either of their proportions; for thus they appear like wit and beauty in the same person.

Henry Purcell
Seventeenth century

Francis Poulenc

THE setting to music of a poem must be an act of love, never a marriage of convenience.

IN order for the contemporary inquirer to understand the music of pre-Constantinian Christianity it is necessary to think cross-culturally. The first Christians lived in a world very different from our own: a world dissimilar not only in time and geography, but distinctive in the ways that its inhabitants perceived and talked about reality. Any attempt to understand early Christian worship music, therefore, requires more than simply learning a new vocabulary or developing an ability to reconcile divergent texts about music in the ancient world. Rather, it compels us to think differently about music and its relationship to the ritual. In doing so we will discover that some contemporary categories — such as distinctions between music and speech — are anachronistic frameworks that the ancients did not employ. Furthermore, many contemporary practices, such as our ability to celebrate worship without music, would be completely unintelligible to Christians of the first centuries. In order to enter into the world of early Christianity and comprehend the place and function of music in that world, we have to imagine and penetrate an auditory environment

Edward Foley   very different from our own.

F OR all its grandeur, there is something greater than music. At Sinai we heard thunder and lightning, but it was not the music of the elements but the word, for the sake of which the great event happened. The Voice goes on forever, and we are being pursued by it. We have neither icons nor statues in our synagogue. We are not even in need of visible symbols to create in us a mood of worship. All we have are words in the liturgy and reverence in our hearts. But even these two are often apart from each other. It is the task of music to bring them together.

Abraham Heschel

I N the beginning was the Word, and the Word was with God, and the Word was God. He was in the beginning with God. All things came into being through him, and without him not one thing came into being. What has come into being in him was life, and the life was the light of all people. The light shines in the darkness, and the darkness did not overcome it.

John 1:1–5

PRAISE *the Lord with the lyre, make melody to him with the harp of ten strings! Sing to him a new song.* Rid yourself of what is old and worn out, for you know a new song. A new man, a new covenant—a new song. This new song does not belong to the old man. Only the new man learns it: the man restored from his fallen condition through the grace of God, and now sharing in the new covenant, that is, the kingdom of heaven. To it all our love now aspires and sings a new song. Let us sing a new song not with our lips but with our lives.

Sing to him a new song, sing to him with joyful melody. Every one of us tries to discover how to sing to God. You must sing to him, but you must sing well. He does not want your voice to come harshly to his ears, so sing well.

If you were asked, "Sing to please this musician," you would not like to do so without having taken some instruction in music, because you would not like to offend an expert in the art. An untrained listener does not notice the faults a musician would point out to you. Who, then, will offer to sing well for God, the great artist whose discrimination is faultless, whose attention is on the minutest detail, whose ear nothing escapes? When will you be able to offer him a perfect performance that you will in no way displease such a supremely discerning listener?

See how he himself provides you with a way of singing. Do not search for words, as if you could find a lyric which would give God pleasure. Sing to him "with songs of joy." This is singing well to God, just singing with songs of joy.

But how is this done? You must first understand that words cannot express the things that are sung by the heart. Take the case of people singing while harvesting in the fields or in the vineyards or when any other strenuous work is in progress. Although they begin by giving expression to their happiness in sung words, yet shortly there is a change. As if so happy that words can no longer express what they feel, they discard the restricting syllables. They burst out into a simple sound of joy, of jubilation. Such a cry of joy is a sound signifying that the heart is bringing to birth what it cannot utter in words.

Now, who is more worthy of such a cry of jubilation than God himself, whom all words fail to describe? If words will not serve, and yet you must not remain silent, what else can you do but cry out for joy? Your heart must rejoice beyond words, soaring into an immensity of gladness, unrestrained by syllabic bonds. *Sing to him with songs of joy.*

Augustine
Fifth century

IN addition to expressing texts, music can also unveil a dimension of meaning and feeling, a communication of ideas and intuitions which words alone cannot yield. This dimension is integral to the human personality and to growth in faith. It cannot be ignored if the signs of worship are to speak to the whole person. Ideally, every communal celebration of faith, including funerals and the sacraments of baptism, confirmation, penance, anointing, and matrimony, should include music and singing.

Music in Catholic Worship

THE wonderful thing about music is that through it one can achieve concentration and meditation independently of thought. In this sense, it bridges the gulf between conscious and unconscious, between form and formlessness. If there is one thing that can be grasped by the understanding and is effective, yet at the same time has no form, that thing is music.

Poetry suggests form; line and color suggest form; but not music. Rather does it create a resonance which vibrates through the whole of the inner and outer universe and transcends all notions of the denseness of matter. Music can even transform matter into spirit, into its original state, by touching every atom of a whole, living being, through the law of harmonic vibration.

The beauty of drawing and painting can go a long way; but it has its limits. The joy of scents and perfumes goes even further. But music penetrates our innermost depths and thus creates a new life-force, a breath of air that lends joy to all existence and leads one's whole being to perfection. Therein lies the fulfillment of human life.

Hazrat Inayat Khan

A ND so, by rhythm and cadence, the poet pretends that his words bring into existence the substance of what they express. The dancer portrays a new mode of existence, entirely free. The painter gives form and color to the invisible, and the musician, in the sonorous language of sound evolved by his own spirit, speaks of realities which transcend speech.

Joseph Gelineau

M ARIE did not think in words as Marcel did. She did not talk to the mirror, nor write out "thoughts" on paper, and even in the Cathedral where she often went alone on Saturday afternoons to kneel for an hour in a pew nearest the altar of the Virgin Mary, there was no outpouring of her soul that was articulate, she did not pray in words.

And those rote prayers she uttered at such times — as she did each morning and each night and with the ringing of the Angelus, or when the beads of her rosary passed through her hands — those rote prayers had precisely that effect they were intended to have when invented centuries and centuries before: they ceased to be language and merely became sound, a rhythmic repetitious sound that lulled the mind and slowly allowed it to empty itself. So that divorced from what others call thought it was free to know itself in terms of the infinite, in terms of that which language has only begun to approximate if not destroy.

Anne Rice

WHO is there that, in logical words, can express the effect music has on us? [A kind of inarticulate, unfathomable speech, which leads us to the edge of the Infinite and lets us for moments gaze into that!]

Sir Thomas Carlyle

PERHAPS, said Kretschmar, it was music's deepest wish not to be heard at all, nor even seen, nor yet felt: but only — if that were possible — in some Beyond, the other side of sense and sentiment, to be perceived and contemplated as pure mind, pure spirit.

Thomas Mann

MY Beloved is the mountains,
And lonely wooded valleys,
Strange islands,
And resounding rivers,
The whistling of love-stirring breezes,

The tranquil night
At the time of the rising dawn,
Silent music,
Sounding solitude,
The supper that refreshes, and deepens love.

John of the Cross
Sixteenth century

O NCE again the music is measured by silence.

Christ is in the tomb as he was in his mother's womb, and just as that first silence was part of the rhythm that moved forward to the visible coming of Life into the world, this silence in the tomb carries the music forward in three great beats to the hour when Life shall again come out of darkness and sweeten and sanctify the world.

Now, as the music becomes audible again, it returns to its simplest form once more. It is lyrical again; at first only a man's breath stirring the flowers in a garden; and then a single word, the name of a friend spoken with indescribable love.

Caryll Houselander

T RY as we may to make a silence, we cannot.

John Cage

N OTHING is more conducive to a communion with the living God than a meditative common prayer with, as its high point, singing that never ends and that continues in the silence of one's heart when one is alone again.

Brother Roger of Taizé

IN a sense, our liturgy is a higher form of silence. It is pervaded by an awed sense of the grandeur of God which resists description and surpasses all expression. The individual is silent. We do not bring forth our own words. Our saying the consecrated words is in essence an act of listening to what they convey. *The Spirit of Israel speaks, the self is silent.*

Twofold is the meaning of silence. One, the abstinence from speech, the absence of sound. Two, inner silence, the absence of self concern, stillness. One may articulate words with the voice and yet be inwardly silent. One may abstain from uttering any sound and yet be overbearing.

Both are inadequate: our speech as well as our silence. Yet there is a level that goes beyond both: the level of song. "There are three ways in which one expresses deep sorrow: the person on the lowest level cries; the person on the second level is silent; the person on the highest level knows how to turn sorrow into song." True prayer is a song.

Abraham Heschel

Some say one should psalmodise often, others — not often, again others — not at all. But I advise you neither to psalmodise so frequently as to cause unrest, nor to leave it off altogether, lest you fall into weakness and negligence, but to follow the example of those who psalmodise infrequently. For, in the words of simple wisdom, moderation is best in all things. To psalmodise much is good for those who follow active life, since they are ignorant of mental occupations and lead a life of labor. But it is not good for those who practice silence, for whom it is more fitting to abide in God alone, praying in their heart and refraining from thought. For, according to John of the Ladder, silence means setting aside thoughts about things, whether of the senses or the mind. Moreover, if it uses up all its energy in too much psalmody, the mind will not have force enough steadily and patiently to remain in prayer. John of the Ladder further advises that at night it is better to give more time to prayer and less to psalmody. — So also must you do. When, sitting in your cell, you see that prayer is acting and does not cease its movement in your heart, never abandon it to get up for psalmody, until it leaves you of its own accord. For otherwise, leaving God within, you will address yourself to Him from without, thus passing from the higher to the lower. Moreover, in this way you will disturb the mind, and remove it from its peaceful calm. Silence, in accord with its name, has in itself such actions as work in peace and quiet. For our God is peace, being above all speech and tumult.

Gregory of Sinai
Fourteenth century

To drop some golden orb of perfect song into our deep, dear silence.

Elizabeth Barrett
Browning
Nineteenth century

IN the ancient days there was a great lord who, feeling himself near to his ending, admonished his only daughter.

"The green of the plum tree has come and gone. Now is the time of blossoming. But still you have not chosen a husband. This and that suitor comes and goes but none is to your liking. Must I die and leave you unaccompanied?"

"Not so, my father," said the Lady Yumiyo. "I shall cause to be fashioned a drum of silk — of silk stretched upon a bamboo frame. He who hears the note when my fingers strike it is the man whom I shall marry."

"This is foolishness," her father said. "A silken drum will make no sound. Alas, I shall never see a grandchild."

But the drum, nevertheless, was made. And many a one came to listen, head stretched forward, urgent to hear — some because of the lady's beauty, some for the readiness of her wit, some because it was widely known that she would be well-provided. And some for all three reasons.

But not a sound did anyone hear when she struck the drum with her hand.

"I told you so," her father said.

But the Lady Yumiyo said nothing. She merely went on striking the drum as the suitors came and went.

And then, one day, in the frame of the doorway, there appeared a well-set-up young man, richly appareled, keen of glance, with the air of one who had come a long way.

He made a deep bow to the old lord and a lesser one to his daughter.

"From where do you come?" the father asked.

"From beyond the mountains and seas and valleys."

"And for what have you come, man from afar?"

"For your daughter, the Lady Yumiyo."

"She is for him who can hear the silk drum. Never tell me that the sound has reached you, across the seas and mountains!"

"No sound of the drum has reached me, sir."

"Then why, stranger, linger here?"

"I have heard its silence," the young man said.

The Lady Yumiyo smiled at her father and put the silken drum aside. She had no longer any need of it.   P. L. Travers

THE temple bell
stops ringing
but the sound keeps
coming
out of the flowers

Matsuo Basho
Seventeenth century

THE notes I handle no better than many pianists. But
the pauses between the notes — ah, that is where the
art resides.

Artur Schnabel

QUITE spontaneously I have used silence as a means of
expression (don't laugh). It is perhaps the only means
of bringing into relief the emotional value of a phrase.

Claude Debussy
Nineteenth century

THERE'S no music in a 'rest,' Katie, that I know of: but there's
the making of music in it. And people are always missing
that part of the life-melody.

John Ruskin
Nineteenth century

For everything there is a season, and a time for every matter under heaven:

a time to be born, and a time to die;

a time to plant, and a time to pluck up what is planted;

a time to kill, and a time to heal;

a time to break down, and a time to build up;

a time to weep, and a time to laugh;

a time to mourn, and a time to dance;

a time to throw away stones, and a time
    to gather stones together;

a time to embrace, and a time to refrain from embracing;

a time to seek, and a time to lose;

a time to keep, and a time to throw away;

a time to tear, and a time to sew;

a time to keep silence, and a time to speak;

a time to love, and a time to hate;

a time for war, and a time for peace.

Ecclesiastes 3:1–8

After silence, that which comes nearest to expressing the inexpressible is music.

Aldous Huxley

WHEN a great crowd gathered and people from town after town came to him, he said in a parable: "A sower went out to sow his seed; and as he sowed, some fell on the path and was trampled on, and the birds of the air ate it up. Some fell on the rock; and as it grew up, it withered for lack of moisture. Some fell among thorns, and the thorns grew with it and choked it. Some fell into good soil, and when it grew, it produced a hundredfold." As he said this, he called out, "Let anyone with ears to hear listen!"

Luke 8:4 – 8

ALL my concerts had no sounds in them; they were completely silent. People had to make their own music in their minds.

Yoko Ono

OH Providence — do but grant me one day of pure joy — For so long now the inner echo of real joy has been unknown to me — Oh when — oh when, Almighty God — shall I be able to hear and feel this echo again in the temple of Nature and in contact with humanity — Never? — No! — Oh, that would be too hard.

Ludwig van Beethoven
Nineteenth century

GREAT art presupposes the alert mind of the educated listener.

Arnold Schoenberg

A song that is well and artificially made cannot be well perceived nor understood at the first hearing, but the oftener you shall hear it, the better cause of liking you will discover, and commonly that song is best esteemed with which our ears are best acquainted.

William Byrd
Seventeenth century

WE hear too much music . . . Until we have a great listening public, and not just a passively *hearing* one, we will never be a musically cultured nation.

Leonard Bernstein

ANY music you hear is made up of time and tone and energy, but there is far more going on than physics. Music needs an initiator and a responder. It is a language sent and received, and for us as humans it is as varied as our human societies. Each aboriginal tribe developed its own language, customs, beliefs and art forms. In music, sounds of nature provided the model: wind and water, bird, fish, animal. Imitating these sounds, primitive people explored their own voices and body sounds, inventing instruments to extend the possibilities. (Flutes and drums of all kinds are common to early societies.) Humans have to learn through their senses, and the arts are exaltations of those senses.

Alice Parker

THE formation of scales and of the web of harmony is a product of artistic invention, and is in no way given by the natural structure or by the natural behaviour of our hearing, as used to be generally maintained hitherto.

Hermann von
Helmholtz
Nineteenth century

MUSIC is natural law as related to the sense of hearing.

Anton von Webern

TRUE music is for the ear alone; a fine voice is the most universal thing that can be figured . . . Accordingly he always used to shut his eyes while hearing music; thereby to concentrate his whole being on the single pure enjoyment of the ear.

Johann Wolfgang
von Goethe
Eighteenth century

THOSE who maintain that they only enjoy music to the full with their eyes shut do not hear better than when they have them open, but the absence of visual distractions enables them to abandon themselves to the reveries induced by the lullaby of its sounds, and that is really what they prefer to the music itself.

Igor Stravinsky

WARBLE, child, make passionate my sense of hearing.

William Shakespeare
Sixteenth century

MUSIC is an innocent luxury, unnecessary, indeed, to our existence, but a great improvement and gratification of the sense of hearing. It consists, at present, of MELODY, TIME, CONSONANCE, and DISSONANCE.

Charles Burney
Eighteenth century

Certain people are affected by religious melodies, and when they come under the influence of melodies which fill the soul with religious excitement they are calmed and restored as if they had undergone a medical treatment and purging. The same sort of effect will also be produced on those who are specially subject to feelings of fear, and pity, or to feelings of any kind.

Aristotle
Fourth century BCE

Elisha said to the king of Israel, "What have I to do with you? Go to your father's prophets or to your mother's." But the king of Israel said to him, "No; it is the LORD who has summoned us; three kings, only to be handed over to Moab." Elisha said, "As the LORD of hosts lives, whom I serve, were it not that I have regard for King Jehosaphat of Judah, I would give you neither a look nor a glance. But get me a musician." And then, while the musician was playing, the power of the LORD came on him. And he said, "Thus says the LORD, 'I will make this wadi full of pools.' For thus says the LORD, 'You shall see neither wind nor rain, but the wadi shall be filled with water, so that you shall drink, you, your cattle, and your animals.' This is only a trifle in the sight of the LORD, for he will also hand Moab over to you. You shall conquer every fortified city and every choice city; every good tree you shall fell, all springs of water you shall stop up, and every good piece of land you shall ruin with stones." The next day, about the time of the morning offering, suddenly water began to flow from the direction of Edom, until the country was filled with water.

2 Kings 3:13–20

WHAT tears I shed in your hymns and canticles! How deeply was I moved by the voices of your sweet singing Church! Those voices flowed into my ears and the truth was distilled into my heart, which overflowed with my passionate devotion. Tears ran from my eyes and happy I was in those tears.

Augustine
Fifth century

SOMETIMES Francis would act in the following way. When the sweetest melody of spirit would bubble up in him, he would give exterior expression to it in French, and the breath of the divine whisper which his ear perceived in secret would burst forth in French in a song of joy. At times, as we saw with our own eyes, he would pick up a stick from the ground and putting it over his left arm, would draw across it, as across a violin, a little bow bent by means of a string; and going through the motions of playing, he would sing in French about his Lord. This whole ecstasy of joy would often end in tears and his song of gladness would be dissolved in compassion for the passion of Christ. Then this saint would bring forth continual sighs, and amid deep groanings, he would be raised up to heaven, forgetful of the lower things he held in his hand.

Thomas of Celano
Thirteenth century

A musical performance also softens hard hearts, leads in the humor of reconciliation, and summons the Holy Spirit.

Hildegard of Bingen
Twelfth century

IN truth we know by experience that song has great force and vigour to move and inflame the hearts of men to invoke and praise God with a more vehement and ardent zeal.

John Calvin
Sixteenth century

THERE let the pealing organ blow
To the full-voiced choir below,
In service high and anthems clear,
As may with sweetness, through mine ear,
Dissolve me into ecstasies,
And bring all heaven before mine eyes.
And may at last my weary age
Find out the peaceful hermitage,
The hairy gown and mossy cell,
Where I may sit and rightly spell
Of every star that heaven doth shew,
And every herb that sips the dew,
Till old experience do attain
To something like prophetic strain.
These pleasures, Melancholy, give,
And I with thee will choose to live.

John Milton
Seventeenth century

Music was as vital as the church edifice itself, more deeply stirring than all the glory of glass or stone. Many a stoic soul, doubtful of the creed, was melted by the music, and fell on his knees before the mystery that no words could speak.   Will Durant

As you come to the town, you will meet a band of prophets coming down from the shrine with harp, tambourine, flute, and lyre playing in front of them; they will be in a prophetic frenzy. Then the spirit of the LORD will possess you, and you will be in a prophetic frenzy along with them and be turned into a different person. Now when these signs meet you, do whatever you see fit to do, for God is with you. And you shall go down to Gilgal ahead of me; then I will come down to you to present burnt offerings and offer sacrifices of well-being. Seven days you shall wait, until I come to you and show you what you shall do.   1 Samuel 10:5–8

Music the fiercest grief can charm,
And Fate's severest rage disarm:
Music can soften pain to ease,
And make despair and madness please:
Our joys below it can improve,   Alexander Pope
And antedate the bliss above.   Eighteenth century

GREAT music is a physical storm, agitating to fathomless depths the mystery of the past within us. Or we might say that it is a prodigious incantation. There are tones that call up all ghosts of youth and joy and tenderness; — there are tones that evoke all phantom pains of perished passion; — there are tones that revive all dead sensations of majesty and might and glory, — all expired exultations, — all forgotten magnanimities. Well may the influence of music seem inexplicable to the man who idly dreams that his life began less than a hundred years ago! He who has been initiated into the truth knows that to every ripple of melody, to every billow of harmony, there answers within him, out of the Sea of Death and Birth, some eddying immeasurable of ancient pleasure and pain.

Paul Elmer More

THE tune came again, like a touch from a small hand that he had unwittingly pushed away. Loch lay back and let it persist. All at once tears rolled out of his eyes. He opened his mouth in astonishment. Then the little tune seemed the only thing in the whole day, the whole summer, the whole season of his fevers and chills, that was accountable: it was personal. But he could not tell why it was so.

It came like a signal, or a greeting — the kind of theme a horn would play out in the woods. He halfway closed his eyes. It came and trailed off and was lost in the neighborhood air. He heard it and then wondered how it went.

Eudora Welty

PRESENTLY, on the other side, the notes of a piano were wakened to the music of a hymn, and the voices of many children took up the air and words. How stately, how comfortable was the melody! How fresh the youthful voices! Markheim gave ear to it smilingly, as he sorted out the keys; and his mind was thronged with answerable ideas and images; church-going children and the pealing of the high organ; children afield, bathers by the brookside, ramblers on the brambly common, kite-flyers in the windy and cloud-navigated sky; and then, at another cadence of the hymn, back again to church, and the somnolence of summer Sundays, and the high genteel voice of the parson (which he smiled a little to recall) and the painted Jacobean tombs, and the dim lettering of the Ten Commandments in the chancel.

Robert Louis
Stevenson
Nineteenth century

GIVE me excess of it, that, surfeiting,
The appetite may sicken, and so die.
That strain again! it had a dying fall:
O! it came o'er my ear like the sweet sound
That breathes upon a bank of violets,
Stealing and giving odor!

William Shakespeare
Sixteenth century

SHE had never before heard such elaborate virtuosity, and never before had she found a piece of music to be so full of surprises. There were sudden, flashing tremolos at the beginning of bars, and places where the music hesitated without losing its tempo, or sustained the same speed despite appearing to halve or double it. Best of all, there were places where a note so high in pitch that it could barely be sounded descended at exhilarating pace down through the scale, and fell upon a reverberant bass note that barely had time to ring before there came a sweet alternation of bass and treble. It made her want to dance or do something foolish.

She watched wonderingly as the fingers of his left hand crawled like a powerful and menacing spider up and down the diapason. She saw the tendons moving and rippling beneath the skin, and then she saw that a symphony of expressions was passing over his face; at times serene, at times suddenly furious, occasionally smiling, from time to time stern and dictatorial, and then coaxing and gentle. Transfixed by this, she realized suddenly that there was something about music that had never been revealed to her before: it was not merely the production of sweet sound; it was, to those who understood it, an emotional and intellectual odyssey. She watched his face, and forgot to attend any more to the music; she wanted to share the journey. She leaned forward and clasped her hands as though she were at prayer.

Louis de Bernières

THAT which colours the mind is a raga.

Sanskrit proverb

Nothing is more characteristic of human nature than to be soothed by sweet modes and stirred up by their opposites. Infants, youths, and old people as well are so naturally attuned to musical modes by a kind of spontaneous feeling that no age is without delights in sweet song.

Boethius
Sixth century

Now the spirit of the Lord departed from Saul, and an evil spirit from the Lord tormented him. And Saul's servant said to him, "See now, an evil spirit from God is tormenting you. Let our lord now command the servants who attend you to look for someone who is skillful in playing the lyre; and when the evil spirit from God is upon you, he will play it, and you will feel better." So Saul said to his servants, "Provide for me someone who can play well, and bring him to me." One of the young men answered, "I have seen a son of Jesse the Bethlehemite who is skillful in playing, a man of valor, a warrior, prudent in speech, and a man of good presence; and the Lord is with him." So Saul sent messengers to Jesse, and said, "Send me your son David who is with the sheep." Jesse took a donkey loaded with bread by his son David to Saul. And David came to Saul, and entered his service. Saul loved him greatly, and he became his armor-bearer. Saul sent to Jesse saying, "Let David remain in my service, for he has found favor in my sight." And whenever the evil spirit from God came upon Saul, David took the lyre and played it with his hand, and Saul would be relieved and feel better, and the evil spirit would depart from him.

1 Samuel 16:14–23

Snowbird Statement
on Catholic
Liturgical Music

BEAUTY is an effective — even sacramental — sign of God's presence and action in the world. The beautiful expresses the joy and delight which prefigure the glory of the liturgy of the heavenly Jerusalem.

Paul Philibert

THE creative disbelief of Nietzche in the last century has helped many theologians understand the dialectical tension within which the contemporary worshiper stands. This is representative of Nietzche's challenge to the church: "For me to believe in their redeemer, Christians would have to sing better songs, and they would have to look more redeemed." Such a complaint helps us see that the tension between performance and participation cannot be collapsed; they must be melded. Performance — the excellence of singing and saying and doing — and participation — the individual's surrender to the transforming work of the worshiping community — must coalesce. One without the other can only be either estheticism or boosters. Together, they become the enfleshment of a mystery that remains age after age both challenge and promise, surrender and consolation.

I T is not the fact that music is a specialized ministry in liturgical celebration which demands the leadership, help, support and strength of professionals. Many specialized ministries are handled well by volunteers, because they concern themselves simply with the proper and effective rendering of what is given them — a function, a text, a pattern of action. The demands of the art of music in our rites exceed immeasurably the demand of other specialized ministries, excepting only that of the presiding minister and preacher (where we also rely on professional commitment). A living church with a living liturgy employing living arts desires and needs, from at least some of its musicians, much more than mere vocal or instrumental competency.   Robert Hovda

T HE pious in every age have considered it a privilege as well as a duty to sing; and they should never be required to relinquish that privilege, except in those cases where individual enjoyment comes in competition with the general interests of devotion.   Thomas Hastings

G IVE thanks for music-making art,
     and praise the Spirit's choice
of members called and set apart
     with instrument and voice.
With work and wisdom, skills hard-won,
life-giving and life-long,
     they celebrate what God has done,
        and lead the people's song.

Through years of training they accrue
     the skills of mind and hand,
which hours of practice must renew,
     enliven, and expand.
With Spirit-grace they tune our hopes;
to Christ their hearts belong;
     for love of God must guide the arts
        that lead the people's song.

With music, moving on through time
     in sequences of sound,
the old, unfolding covenant
of justice righting wrong,
     resounds through word and sacrament,
        and leads the people's song.

Then let us reach for excellence
    to sing and symphonize
for God, our utmost audience,
    with joy our highest prize.
When kindly skill our spirit lifts
and makes the humble strong,
        give thanks, and praise the graceful gifts
            that lead the people's song.

God, give us music to express
    and richly interweave
our yearning with our thankfulness,
    and sing what we believe,
till, glorious in the realms of grace,
with new creation's throng,
        our Savior meets us face to face
            and leads the people's song.   Brian Wren

O̲UR limits and sins impose such ugliness upon the
world; public worship should reveal its beauty in
every way it can.   Robert Hovda

MUSICIANS concerned with the liturgy require something in addition to their musical background and the scientific knowledge of church legislation, rubrics and ceremonial. Above all, they must have the spirit of the liturgy, enthusiasm for the true understanding of the liturgy. They must have some insight into the truths of theology and be possessed with the deep spirituality underlying the liturgical services because organist and choir director take such a prominent part in them. A prayerful, reverent sense of the mystery must be in the minds and in the hearts of those who have to watch every step of the liturgical services. Supernatural awareness must be a prerequisite for anyone who conducts a liturgical service. The dryness of routine and repetition and the dullness of spirit which may overtake church musicians must be opposed by prayerful reading and serious study. Without spiritual, intellectual food, liturgical musicians will become dull automatons. Only a great, inspired teacher will be able to inspire others.

Josephine Morgan

EVERY sound in worship is, at its root, musical. The tunefulness of worship, therefore, is not confined to the sounding of instruments or to the vocalization of choirs or other musical specialists. Liturgy is to be tuneful in every human sound, including speech.

Milwaukee Symposia for Church Composers

JUNE 12, 1980: The Leprosarium on Guimaras. So it was St. Alice's Day, the feast of the thirteenth-century mystic and leper. Since this feast is, appropriately enough, the patronal feast of the leprosarium, much of the day's activity in the spacious compound was being directed toward the preparations for the coming feast. In one of the large barrack-wards, Sr. Marie introduced Fr. Fabian and me to some of the men who were preparing their music for the next day's celebration. There were three of them, each with his own musical instrument. The instruments themselves had been fashioned with great love, skill and ingenuity by one of the members of the trio. A musicologist would have a bit of difficulty, I admit, in classifying each of these instruments, probably settling for something generic, like "a guitar-like string instrument." But each of these instruments was the work of a true craftsman. What stuck deepest, however, was the music itself, or rather, the musicians. I doubt that the three players had between them four whole fingers. Their hands ended mostly in knobs and stubs. What kind of music can you play with one finger, a knuckle-bone and a few stubs? Not one of the three was physically able to negotiate more than a few notes and chord-sequences. And yet, by pooling their limited resources, and by each contributing his own limited efforts, these men were playing and singing music, *real* music, *beautiful* music. It may not have been Bach or Beethoven. But I can assure you that Bach or Beethoven would have deemed themselves privileged to join these three lepers in their music-making.

If the highly gifted (or even the moderately gifted!) individuals can exercise their gifts at liturgy for the sake of the community, splendid! But even more important is the willingness of the rest of us, those of us with only stubs and knobs instead of fingers, to join with others like ourselves. Within such a matrix a community liturgy has every chance of flourishing.

Chrysogonus Waddell

Martin Luther
Sixteenth century

THE devil does not stay where music is.

OUR society is perhaps the only one known to have separated the best music-making from religion and so to have allowed an inferior strain of functional music to usurp the place of all-uniting sound. It is interesting but fruitless to speculate on who initiated the divorce. In a way we are all responsible. The separation of music itself into different spheres—high art, academic, folk, pop, jazz, religious—is symptomatic of twentieth-century stresses.

Alice Parker

MAKING aesthetic judgments based on your own musical understanding is not adequate because what has candor to us may not appear that way to people in the congregation. We have to learn how to make these judgments for groups of people whose life of faith is as wide-ranging as their musical tastes. Our task is to find, or write, good music that is expressive of the life of faith of the congregation. To do so means learning about the musical and faith lives of the people in the pews. Fortunately, the two go together: Learning the music of people *is* learning their faith. Musician and congregation join in a mutual education project, in which a variety of musical expressions are shared among people of different ages, cultures, and traditions.

Linda J. Clark

IN the past the rubrics scarcely concerned themselves with the community itself; all the attention went into seeing that the chant conformed not to the spirit of a people but to the letter of rubrical laws. All the Christian communities throughout the world were made to sing the same Gregorian melodies, for example, the triple Alleluia of the Vigil Mass of Easter, whether they liked it or not. Indian Christians might have protested: "We don't like this melody. We prefer to sing music written in the five notes of our own musical scale. How beautiful are our five notes! But the seven notes of your Western scale and that Alleluia appear vulgar to us, as ridiculous as if a young Indian woman should dress in European style, in shorts or in slacks!" The rubrics would reply: "No matter! You must sing it nevertheless, as it is written!" Christians in the African bush might implore: "Let's have a bit more rhythm please for this Alleluia! For rhythm is our joy, through which we love to sing praise to the risen Christ. But your Alleluia resembles a burial chant!" The rubrics would reply: "No matter! You must sing it as it is written!" Christians in the suburbs might say: "We are not able to sing this Alleluia together as an expression of the union of our hearts. Rather, it reduces us to silence, as our voices slide and slip on the notes as if on ice." Again, the rubrics would reply: "No matter! You must sing it as it is written!"   Lucien Deiss

WHAT wondrous love is this,
O my soul, O my soul?
What wondrous love is this, O my soul?
What wondrous love is this
that caused the Lord of bliss
To bear the dreadful curse for my soul, for my soul;
To bear the dreadful curse for my soul?

To God and to the Lamb
I will sing, I will sing;
To God and to the Lamb, I will sing;
To God and to the Lamb
who is the great I Am,
While millions join the theme, I will sing, I will sing;
While millions join the theme, I will sing.

And when from death I'm free,
I'll sing on, I'll sing on;
And when from death I'm free, I'll sing on;
And when from death I'm free,
I'll sing and joyful be,
And through eternity I'll sing on, I'll sing on!
And through eternity I'll sing on.

Alexander Means
Nineteenth century

How good to thank you, LORD,
to praise your name, Most High,
to sing your love at dawn,
your faithfulness at dusk
with sound of lyre and harp,
with music of the lute.
For your work brings delight,
your deeds invite song.

Psalm 92:2–5

AFTER Israel has crossed the sea through the mighty power of God, Miriam leads them in song. After great victories over powerful foes, Deborah and Judith sing God's praises. Hezekiah sings his thanksgiving after he is delivered from illness. It seems natural for God's people, whenever they experience God's action in their lives, to burst into song.

Irene Nowell

THOSE who wish to sing always find a song.

Swedish proverb

SING to the LORD a new song,
the LORD of wonderful deeds.
Right hand and holy arm
brought victory to God.

God made that victory known,
revealed justice to the nations,
remembered a merciful love
loyal to the house of Israel.
The ends of the earth have seen
the victory of our God.

Shout to the LORD, you earth,
break into song, into praise!
Sing praise to God with a harp,
with a harp and sound of music.
With sound of trumpet and horn,
shout to the LORD, our king.

Psalm 98:1–6

IN the dark times
Will there also be singing?
Yes, there will also be singing
About the dark times.

Bertolt Brecht

THERE is delight in singing, tho' none hear beside the
singer.

Walter Savage Landor
Nineteenth century

SING God a simple song:
Lauda, Laude.
Make it up as you go along:
Lauda, Laude . . .
Sing like you like to sing.
God loves all simple things,
For God is the simplest of all,
For God is the simplest of all.

Stephen Schwartz and
Leonard Bernstein

ABOUT midnight Paul and Silas were praying and singing hymns to God, and the prisoners were listening
to them.

Acts 16:25

SINGING is a noble art and good exercise. It has nothing
to do with worldly affairs, with the strife of the market
place and the rivalries of the court. The singer fears no evil;
he forgets all worry and is happy.

Martin Luther
Sixteenth century

Gabe Huck

IT is not only this one ritual of ours — Sunday eucharist — that has its music, that must be sung. All sorts of regular moments, recurring moments, have had their songs, their tunes, their sounds. Do they still? Do they have these not as nostalgia and not as entertainment but as their own, as the very way we rock a baby, walk a picket line, begin a morning, end a year, keep a festival?

Gerard Pottebaum

WHEN we look at ourselves through a visiting scientist's eyes, we can see that people in a technological culture still enjoy traditional rituals. No effort is made by organizations, institutions, or churches to perpetuate these rites. No religious education program is organized to teach the sequence of events, the proper way to cut the cake, or the melody to the song.

West African proverb

WITHOUT a song the bush-knife is dull.

WHEN music wakes my sleeping heart
and plays my spirit strong,
then all I love is gracious gift
and every breath, a song.

When music gathers us in prayer
and summons us to praise,
then beauty spills her shining light
across our darkened days.

When music fills the universe
and all is melody,
then Christ the Lord will lead a hymn
of soaring majesty:

"All honor to the Holy One,
all praise and glory be!"
Our alleluias without end
will ring in harmony.

Delores Dufner

'TIS a sure sign that work goes on merrily, when folks sing
at it.

Isaac Bickerstaffe
Eighteenth century

WHEN you go to war in your land against the adver-
sary who oppresses you, you shall sound an alarm
with the trumpets, so that you may be remembered before
the LORD your God and be saved from your enemies.

Numbers 10:9

W E cannot be whole without music. Music is not a decoration applied to the liturgy, like icing on a cake. Music is not an ornament on a liturgy that is substantially intact without it. Music is an integral part of liturgical celebration because it is an integral part of a whole human communication, of a full, rich human celebration.

Robert Hovda

S ACRED music, being an integral part of the liturgy, is directed to the general object of this liturgy, namely, the glory of God and the sanctification and edification of the faithful. It helps to increase the beauty and splendor of the ceremonies of the Church, and since its chief duty is to clothe the liturgical text, which is presented to the understanding of the faithful, with suitable melody, its object is to make that text more efficacious, so that the faithful through this means may be more roused to devotion, and better disposed to gather to themselves the fruits of grace which come from the celebration of the sacred mysteries.

Pope Pius X

A theology of Christian ritual music is necessary if we are to adapt traditional musical forms to a renewed liturgy, to forge new forms and to shape our ritual music so that it is appropriately united to the liturgy. Such a theology is founded on the pastoral conviction that music shapes the relationship of believers to God and to each other.

*Milwaukee Symposia
for Church Composers*

WHEN they had sung the hymn, they went out to the Mount of Olives.

Mark 16:26

THEY affirmed, however, that this was the extent of their fault or error, that they were wont to assemble on a set day before dawn and to sing a hymn among themselves (*carmen. . . . dicere secum invicem*) to the Christ, as to a god, and that they pledged themselves by vow not to some crime, but that they would commit neither fraud, nor theft, nor adultery, nor betray their word, nor deny a trust when summoned; after which it was their custom to separate and to come together again to take food—ordinary and harmless food, however.

Pliny the Younger
First century

THE faithful who gather to await the Lord's coming are urged by the Apostle Paul to sing psalms, hymns, and inspired songs (see Colossians 3:16). Song is the sign of the heart's joy (see Acts 2:46), and Saint Augustine said: "To sing belongs to lovers." Even in antiquity it was proverbial to say, "He prays twice who sings well."

*General Instruction of
the Roman Missal*

O God our Father, we thank you for music and its wondrous power to touch and heal and strengthen; under its spell the closed doors of the human spirit are unlocked and our hearts are moved to respond to you in worship. We praise you for this most precious gift.

We thank you for all those who, entrusted with this gift, have "composed musical tunes and set forth verses in writing"; living on among us in their works, they have wonderfully enriched our lives and exalted you in the liturgy of your Church. We praise you for all faithful singers of your song.

We thank you for all who teach in conservatories and schools of sacred music, interpreting music born in the souls of others and bringing gifts to fruition in many generations of students. We praise you for what they, receiving generously from you, have shared generously with others.

And lastly we thank you for all who day by day enable us to sing your song in many ways and many places, accompanying it on organ and guitar and trumpet, leading it with the beauty of the solo voice, enriching it with new forms of music, patient scholarship and gifted teaching. We praise you for their ministry and gratefully ask your blessing on it this day.

Jeffrey Rowthorn

Liturgical music must be like John the Baptist: always pointing to Christ, never calling attention to itself.

Brother Roger of Taizé

The Apostolic Age bears witness to the joyful character of early Christianity, particularly as it was expressed in singing. In Ephesians 5:19 Paul calls upon Christians to address one another with psalms, hymns and spiritual songs, singing and making melody to the Lord in your heart.

Colossians 3:16 also refers to singing "psalms and hymns and spiritual songs with thankfulness in your hearts to God." These words clearly express the Apostle's conviction that singing is a fitting way to honor God. There is at the same time, however, a certain reservation in what Paul says. In both passages he adds what seems to be a warning against a purely aesthetic pleasure in singing: such singing must take place "in your heart." This articulates well the primitive Christian position on liturgical singing. Only insofar as singing is the expression of an inner disposition of devotion does it have any meaning.

This attitude toward liturgical singing clearly approximated that held by the pagan philosophers previously mentioned. Still, it avoided the exaggerated spiritualistic tendency which regarded music as an obstacle to cultic action and portrayed the renunciation of music in liturgy as the higher ideal. Rather, the characteristics which Paul required of Christian song resulted in a highly spiritualized concept of divine worship. This prevailed to such an extent that Christians in the succeeding era often designated liturgical song as their sacrifice, thus distinguishing it from pagan sacrifice.

Johannes Quasten

B UT it is also possible for this artist to change his creative
ideals by striving primarily to produce a work of art
intended to be admired for its own sake, a precious thing to
win the esteem of connoisseurs, a refined piece which will
stand as an achievement of human skill, irrespective of
whether it is actually used in divine worship or not. The
artistic *chef-d'oeuvre,* thus displayed as an esthetic symbol
of the religious thoughts or sentiments of a culture, will more
naturally find its true place in a museum or concert hall than
in the liturgy. In the celebration of the sacred mysteries no
work of art should set itself up as the aim and object of the
soul's movements; a *chef-d'oeuvre* (masterpiece) which
attracts too much attention to itself runs the risk of looking
like a *hors-d'oeuvre* (digression). The liturgy requires for its
handmaids that they should stimulate "prayer within beauty,"
Joseph Gelineau   not that they should "foster beauty within prayer."

B EWARE the ecclesiastical specialist, whether he or she is
a pope or a teacher or a musician or a writer, who has
a commitment prior to that of the common commitment
of believers.

For the ecclesiastical specialist who is not first and fore-
most a believer, the holy, the sacred, the mystery are identi-
fied too easily with a completed system, a finished church,
a classic form of art — where God is somehow captured and
made static, made secure as our possession, subject to our
control . . . and where the signs of God's great love and
saving care, the sacraments, are entities apart from any
sordid human grasp, splendid in their isolated and unused
Robert Hovda   perfection.

Now we have the resurrection depicted by tremolando passages and more "effects" for six trumpets. Religious music of this sort is only remarkable as naïve blasphemy, wonderfully elaborated, and convinced of its own piety. Doubtless, many of the public are pleased, much as they would be if, on going to church, they found sensational novels bound up in their Bible covers, and were surprised to find Scripture so amusing.

George Bernard Shaw

When in our music God is glorified,
And adoration leaves no room for pride,
It is as though the whole creation cried
Alleluia!

How often, making music, we have found
A new dimension in the world of sound,
As worship moved us to a more profound
Alleluia!

So has the Church in liturgy and song,
In faith and love, through centuries of wrong,
Borne witness to the truth in ev'ry tongue,
Alleluia!

And did not Jesus sing a psalm that night
When utmost evil strove against the Light?
Then let us sing, for whom he won the fight,
Alleluia!

Let ev'ry instrument be tuned for praise!
Let all rejoice who have a voice to raise!
And may God give us faith to sing always
Alleluia! Alleluia!

Fred Pratt Green

THIS holiest day, sing high, sing low,
And let the merry anthem flow,
Benedicamus Domino. Alleluya.

And we, with voice devout and sweet,
Most humbly, as 'tis right and meet,
Will *Deo gratias* repeat. Alleluya.

Jean Tisserand
Fifteenth century

OURS is a singing faith!
Now hear the hymns we raise,
Resounding, strong, the years along,
And echoing our praise.
Ours is a singing faith!
In confidence we sing:
Creation's throne is God's alone,
So joyous voices ring.

Ours is a singing faith!
All thanks to God be sung
By people here both far and near
In every land and tongue.
Ours is a singing faith!
Let psalms and anthems rise
From sun and moon and stars in tune
Till music fills the skies!

Jane Parker Huber

THEREFORE, let us ever remember the words of the prophet: *Serve ye the Lord in fear;* and again, *Sing ye wisely;* and, *In the sight of the angels will I sing to thee.* Let us then consider how we ought to behave ourselves in the presence of God and his angels, and so sing the psalms that mind and voice may be in harmony.

Rule of Saint Benedict

THE joy it is to sing
you praises, God most high,
   sing you thanks for what you
are, at sunrise to your
   love, at sunset and through
the watches of the night
   to your fidelity,
to the pluck of the lyre,
   the zither and the harp.
For you give me joy, God,
   in all the things you do.
My song is about you,
   your immense creation,
your mind too deep to plumb.

Francis Patrick
Sullivan

MY beloved speaks and says to me:
Arise, my love, my fair one,
   and come away;
for now the winter is past,
   the rain is over and gone.
The flowers appear on the earth;
   the time of singing has come,
and the voice of the turtledove
   is heard in our land.

Song of Solomon
2:10–12

Sing, my soul, of waking life!
Dawn is here: Your God revere!
See the Eastern sky aglow;
Hear the sounds of morning grow!
Greet with joy the rising sun:
Day, in splendor, has begun!

Sing a psalm of gratitude;
Glorify the Lord most high!
Nature, bathed in morning's rays,
Chants to God a hymn of praise;
Earth, bejeweled with sparkling dew,
Becket G. Senchur   Welcomes Christ her Light anew!

He [David] appointed certain of the Levites as ministers before the ark of the LORD, to invoke, to thank, and to praise the LORD, the God of Israel. Asaph was the chief, and second to him Zechariah, Jeiel, Shemiramoth, Jehiel, Mattithiah, Eliab, Benaiah, Obed-edom, and Jeiel, with harps and lyres; Asaph was to sound the cymbals, and the priests Benaiah and Jahaziel were to blow trumpets regularly, before the ark of the covenant of God.

Then on that day David first appointed the singing of praises to the LORD by Asaph and his kindred.

O give thanks to the LORD, call on
    his name,
make known his deeds among
    the peoples.
Sing to him, sing praises to him,
1 Chronicles 16:4–9   tell of all his wonderful works.

ADAH bore Jabal; he was the ancestor of those who live
in tents and have livestock. His brother's name was
Jubal; he was the ancestor of all those who play the lyre
and pipe.   Genesis 4:20–21

THE organ is in truth the grandest, the most daring,
the most magnificent of all instruments invented by
human genius.
Surely it is, in some sort, a pedestal on which the soul
poises for a flight into space—   Honoré de Balzac
to cross the infinite that separates Heaven and Earth.   Nineteenth century

REJOICE in the LORD, O you righteous.
Praise befits the upright.
Praise the LORD with the lyre;
make melody to him with the harp of ten strings.
Sing to him a new song;
play skillfully on the strings, with loud shouts.

For the word of the LORD is upright,
and all his work is done in faithfulness.
He loves righteousness and justice;
the earth is full of the steadfast love of the LORD.   Psalm 33:1–5

DESCEND ye Nine! descend and sing;
    The breathing Instruments inspire,
Wake into Voice each silent String,
    And sweep the sounding Lyre!
    In a sadly-pleasing Strain
    Let the warbling Lute complain:
      Let the loud Trumpet sound,
      Till the Roofs all around
      The shrill Echos rebound:
    While in more lengthen'd Notes and slow,
The deep, majestick, solemn Organs blow.
      Hark! the Numbers, soft and clear,
      Gently steal upon the Ear;
      Now louder, and yet louder rise,
      And fill with spreading Sounds the Skies;
Exulting in Triumph now swell the bold Notes,
In broken Air, trembling, the wild Musick floats;
    Till, by degrees, remote and small,
      The Strains decay,
      And melt away
    In a dying, dying Fall.

Alexander Pope
Eighteenth century

To You,
 to You above,
to You above holy
and strong,
be joy,
be joy from us
for boundless lifegiving
power,
joy from
our trumpets, joy
from our lyrical strings,
joy from
our drums
and dances and
harps, pipes, and shivering
cymbals,
joy from
our clashing, our
ringing with all that lives
to You!

Francis Patrick
Sullivan

WHEN a man occupies his time with flutes, stringed instruments, choirs, dancing, Egyptian krotala and other such improper frivolities, he will find that indecency and rudeness are the consequences. Such a man creates a din with cymbals and tambourines; he rages about with instruments of an insane cult. . . . Leave the syrinx to shepherds and the flute to superstitious devotees who rush to serve their idols. We completely forbid the use of these instruments at our temperate banquet.

Clement of Alexandria
Third century

SAUL and David — Soft sounds come upon me through the body of my host. These are plucked from gut by small fingers. They move slowly in persuasive and beautiful tones. From what I can tell, they are the hands and soul of a child. My dark hands are trembling, and the heart of the man I inhabit begins to pulse with a new strength . . . I turn to see the gentle, unhurried boy, his fingers tangled nimbly in the strings of his harp and see the king whom my evil would have killed, turn and behold his small savior.

James Dickey and
Marvin Hayes

SING to God, not with the voice, but with the heart. Although a man be *kakophonos,* to use a common expression, if he have good works, he is a sweet singer before God.

Jerome
Fourth century

THE man that hath no music in himself,
    Nor is not moved to concord of sweet sounds,
is fit for treasons, stratagems and spoils;
The motions of his spirit are dull as night
And his affections dark as Erebus:
Let no such man be trusted. Mark the music.

William Shakespeare
Sixteenth century

So David assembled all Israel from the Shihor of Egypt to Lebo-hamath, to bring the ark of God from Kiriath-jearim. And David and all Israel went up to Baalah, that is, to Kiriath-jearim, which belongs to Judah, to bring up from there the ark of God, the LORD, who is enthroned on the cherubim, which is called by his name. They carried the ark of God on a new cart, from the house of Abinadab, and Uzzah and Ahio were driving the cart. David and all Israel were dancing before God with all their might, with song and lyres and harps and tambourines and cymbals and trumpets.

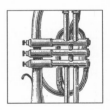

1 Chronicles 13:5–8

G OD guard me from the thoughts men think
In the mind alone;
He that sings a lasting song

William Butler Yeats   Thinks in the marrow-bone.

V *ide ut quod ore cantas, corde credas, et quod corde*
credis, operibus comprobes.

Fourth Council of   Take heed that what you sing with your mouths you believe
Carthage   in your hearts, and what you believe with your hearts you
Fourth century   show forth in your works.

T HERE must be a strenuous attempt to replace music that
comes from the fingers and the mechanical playing of

Zoltán Kodály   instruments with music from the soul and based on singing.

L ET the word of Christ dwell in you richly; teach and
admonish one another in all wisdom; and with gratitude
in your hearts sing psalms, hymns, and spiritual songs to
God. And whatever you do, in word or deed, do everything
in the name of the Lord Jesus, giving thanks to God the

Colossians 3:16–17   Father through him.

THIS won't be a love song till we know the words by heart.   Bob Gibson

So the builders built the temple of the Lord. And the priests stood arrayed in their vestments, with musical instruments and trumpets, and the Levites, the sons of Asaph, with cymbals, praising the Lord and blessing him, according to the directions of King David of Israel; they sang hymns, giving thanks to the Lord, "For his goodness and his glory are forever upon all Israel." And all the people sounded trumpets and shouted with a great shout, praising the Lord for the erection of the house of the Lord. Some of the Levitical priests and heads of ancestral houses, old men who had seen the former house, came to the building of this one with outcries and loud weeping, while many came with trumpets and a joyful noise, so that the people could not hear the trumpets because of the weeping of the people.   Esdras 5:58–65

I have to really feel a song before I'll deal with it, and just about every song I do is based either on an experience I've had or an experience someone I know had gone through.   Aretha Franklin

Leo Tolstoy **M**USIC is the shorthand of emotion.

Myles Connolly **I**F one loves anything, truth, beauty, woman, life, one will speak out. Genuine love cannot endure silence. Genuine love breaks into speech. And when it is great love, it breaks out into song.

1 Maccabees 9:37–42 **A**FTER these things it was reported to Jonathan and his brother Simon, "The family of Jambri are celebrating a great wedding, and are conducting the bride, a daughter of one of the great nobles of Canaan, from Nadabath with a large escort." Remembering how their brother John had been killed, they went up and hid under cover of the mountain. They looked out and saw a tumultuous procession with a great amount of baggage; and the bridegroom came out with his friends and his brothers to meet them with tambourines and musicians and many weapons. Then they rushed on them from the ambush and began killing them. Many were wounded and fell, and the rest fled to the mountain; and the Jews took all their goods. So the wedding was turned into mourning and the voice of their musicians into a funeral dirge. After they had fully avenged the blood of their brother, they returned to the marshes of the Jordan.

I sing to people about what matters. I sing to the realists;
people who accept it like it is. I express problems. There
are tears when it's sad and smiles when it's happy. It seems
simple to me, but to some, feelings take courage.   Aretha Franklin

THE Lord brings us back to Zion,
we are like dreamers,
laughing, dancing,
with songs on our lips.

Other nations say,
"A new world of wonders!
The Lord is with them."
Yes, God works wonders.
Rejoice! Be glad!

Lord, bring us back
as water to thirsty land.
Those sowing in tears
reap, singing and laughing.

They left weeping, weeping,
casting the seed.
They come back singing, singing,
holding high the harvest.   Psalm 126

ISRAEL's earliest lyrical response to the action of God was
praise and thanks. Israel noticed the transformation of its
life and attributed the saving inversion to the power of
Yahweh. They told and retold the narrative of inversion
(Exodus 14). They broke out in song that characterized the
change, and they named the one who worked the change.   Walter Brueggemann

Now Jericho was shut up inside and out because of the Israelites; no one came out and no one went in. The LORD said to Joshua, "See, I have handed Jericho over to you, along with its king and soldiers. You shall march around the city, all the warriors circling the city once. Thus you shall do for six days, with seven priests bearing seven trumpets of rams' horns before the ark. On the seventh day you shall march around the city seven times, the priests blowing the trumpets. When they make a long blast with the ram's horn, as soon as you hear the sound of the trumpet, then all the people shall shout with a great shout; and the wall of the city will fall down flat, and all the people shall charge straight ahead." So Joshua son of Nun summoned the priests and said to them, "Take up the ark of the covenant, and have seven priests carry seven trumpets of rams' horns in front of the ark of the LORD." To the people he said, "Go forward and march around the city; have the armed men pass on before the ark of the LORD."

Joshua 6:1–7

I never said there were not strong political implications to what I did. I just said the music was not overtly political. But the implications of the music certainly are. And I still think it's the most popular form of politics, more powerful than saying it right on the money, in which case you're usually preaching to the converted.

Paul Simon

Through song," said the Rebbe, "you climb to the highest palace. From that palace you can influence the universe and its prisons. Song is Jacob's ladder forgotten on
earth by the angels. Sing and you shall defeat death; sing
and you shall disarm the foe."   Elie Wiesel

My life flows on in endless song
Above earth's lamentation.
I hear the real though far-off hymn
That hails a new creation.

Through all the tumult and the strife,
I hear that music ringing;
It sounds and echoes in my soul;
How can I keep from singing?

What though the tempest 'round me roar,
I hear the truth it liveth.
What though the darkness 'round me close,
Songs in the night it giveth.

When tyrants tremble, sick with fear,
And hear their death knells ringing;
When friends rejoice both far and near,   Traditional Quaker
How can I keep from singing?   hymn

Gabe Huck

SOME might say, "Where's the message?" That's a very good question when we look at texts but not as easy as it appears. Like rite itself, and like all the words of our rites, the words of our songs are not intended to be snappy slogans advertising this spirituality or that gospel-based politics. The good words are those that shape us in light of the gospel and its liturgy, shape and form us in this way: that over the many, many times we sing them they do not wear out but become our own dear and cherished vocabulary. They do all those things that Heschel and Sexton and Updike told us about words. Message? We are the message.

Eric Werner

QUITE in conformity with the ideologies of the entire Near East, music is not so much a thing of beauty as an ethical force.

W<small>E</small> need to perceive that the music can be a tool or vehicle to achieve not only musical literacy but also a host of other important objectives necessary to living in today's world: aesthetic perception and taste, and an awareness of, concern for, and tolerance of one's fellow man — whatever his position in life.

We need to reach into all segments of our society and at all age levels with the message and with demonstrated proof that music can heal many wounds, bring rest to the weary and comfort to the troubled, inspire the latently talented, and draw out the creativity inherent in every person.   Denise Bacon

P<small>EOPLE</small> who make music together cannot be enemies, at least while the music lasts.
                                                                Paul Hindemith

T<small>HEN</small> the prophet Miriam, Aaron's sister, took a tambourine in her hand; and all the women went out after her with tambourines and with dancing. And Miriam sang to them:

"Sing to the L<small>ORD</small>, for he has triumphed gloriously; horse and rider he has thrown into the sea."   Exodus 15:20–21

Gail Ramshaw

Let the words of our hymns be worth singing. Inspired by the metaphors in the psalter, let our hymnals be treasure chests overflowing with such multi-faceted jewels that it is difficult to choose between the diamond and the opal. An excellent hymn, like a great poem, wants to be memorized. You sing it at the liturgy and are delighted, perhaps even astounded, and you sing it over and over that week until you know its words by heart. You want to join in singing the words, for the words themselves sing.

Gail Ramshaw

Several unhelpful tendencies, however, are recurring in the stacks of newly composed hymnody. Some hymns are marked by mediocre scriptural knowledge or erroneous theology. Some are smitten by immature emotion. Some are obsessive "cause songs" which mean to induce in the assembly the estimable attitudes of the hymnwriter. The assembly rightly feels exhausted after participating in such browbeating. Some hymn texts, modeled after twentieth-century poetry, are far too dense to be accessible for the singing congregation. One innovation that deserves absolute censure is the "I am God" hymnody, in which the assembly, pretending to be God, sings some supposed divine words. Those hymns which snuggle up to God as my best buddy might perhaps first kneel before the mystery of the divine. Easy anthropomorphisms lean toward idolatry by depicting God in our own image.

How is it that in matters concerning the flesh we have so many fine poems and hymns but that in those concerning the spirit we have such sluggish, cold affairs?

Martin Luther
Sixteenth century

Those who choose music for liturgy should come to the task disciplined by their engagement with the words of psalms and other texts of the tradition. The test for any text to be sung at liturgy must be both the strength of its poetry and the fidelity (to our scriptures, to our liturgy) of its meaning. No kitsch.

Gabe Huck

Every place we give to inferior and unworthy words is a place not given to strong words.

Gabe Huck

ONE of the earliest books for children was *Divine and Moral Songs* published by Isaac Watts in 1720, and the tone was more moralistic than divine. One of the most widely quoted items is:

Let dogs delight to bark and bite,
For God hath made them so;
Let bears and lions growl and fight,
For 'tis their nature, too.

But, children, you should never let
Such angry passions rise;
Your little hands were never made
To tear each other's eyes.

However, in all fairness we must admit that the following hymn by Watts for children is a gem:

I sing the almighty power of God,
That made the mountains rise;
That spread the flowing seas abroad,
And built the lofty skies.

His hand is my perpetual guard,
He keeps me with his eye;
Why should I then forget the Lord,
Who is forever nigh?

In America the moralistic song flourished in examples such as "Wicked Polly," who, in her deathbed warning to others, catalogues all her wicked ways which now send her to the fiery pits of hell.

The next group of hymn writers were of the "little lamb school." They thought of children as sweet little lambs, and all their examples exude sweetness and light, figuratively patting the little lamb on his head in a patronizing way and talking down to the child. Two things a child despises are to be thought of as little and to be talked down to as an inferior.

The next generation was of the "lollipop school" whose philosophy was to keep the children happy with musical pacifiers. This was the age of the jingly chorus since children "love bright tunes" — according to the theory of that day. "Brighten the corner where you are" is a choice example of this category. Perhaps few of the songs are downright harmful, but nourishment found in "lollipops" is most inadequate spiritual food.

In the last generation the emphasis has been on the teaching possibilities of hymns — the period of the graded curriculum with songs manufactured to fit a particular lesson unit or to achieve a specific goal or response. On the whole this material is better than much that went before, but generally musical settings sound contrived and aesthetic values often take a back seat to pedagogy.

Feeding an individual mere facts, doctrines, dogmas, and catechisms is ineffective in terms of the goals of Christian education and sometimes is invalid unless the feeding results in growth in the Christian life.

Austin C. Lovelace and
William C. Rice

Oscar Wilde
Nineteenth century

THERE seems to be some curious connection between piety and poor rhyme.

IT is difficult but important to demand of our words at liturgy what the culture has practically ceased to ask of all its speakers (advertisers, politicians, teachers, "stars"): passion, simplicity, the capacity to be there again and again to put names on all of reality.

Gabe Huck

Matthew 6:7

WHEN you are praying, do not heap up empty phrases.

THE psalms are rich in imagery, feeling, and symbolism. They powerfully express the suffering and pain, the hope and trust of people of every age and culture. Above all the psalms sing of faith in God, of revelation and redemption. They enable the assembly to pray in the words that Jesus himself used during his life on earth. In the psalms the members of the assembly pray in the voice of Christ, who intercedes on their behalf before the Father. The Church, like Christ, turns again and again to the psalms as a genuine expression of grief and of praise and as a sure source of trust and hope in times of trial.

Order of Christian Funerals

A psalm implies serenity of soul; it is the author of peace. A psalm forms friendships, unites those separated, conciliates those at enmity. A psalm is a city of refuge from the demons; a means of inducing help from the angels, a weapon in fears by night, a rest from toils by day, a safeguard for infants, an adornment for those at the height of their vigor, a consolation for the elders, a most fitting ornament for women. It peoples the solitudes; it rids the market place of excesses; it is the elementary exposition of beginners, the improvement of those advancing, the solid support of the perfect, the voice of the Church. It brightens the feast days; it creates a sorrow which is in accordance with God. For a psalm calls forth a tear even from a heart of stone. A psalm is the work of angels, a heavenly institution, the spiritual incense.

Basil
Fourth century

NOBODY can know and love Western music of the six-teenth through the twentieth centuries without being drenched in settings of the psalms. My very first contact with the ubiquitous Vulgate versions was, again, at grade school, where the same music teacher who taught us "Old Hundredth" gave us the Elizabethan canon on the lines that I would not for many years be able to put together with those that followed on the filling of the fourth cup of wine at seder: *lo lanu adonai lo lanu / ki-lshimkha ten kavod / al hasdkha al-amitekha*. What we sang at school in the Latin I had not yet learned any of was its translation: *non nobis domine, non nobis / sed nomini tuo da gloriam* (Psalm 115:1). By the time I reached college, the Vulgate Psalter was ubiquitous in my musical world. Vivaldi's *"Beatus vir"* setting of Psalm 112 — *Beatus vir qui timet dominum / in mandatus eius volet nimis*—which I read through and wrote liner notes for while at Columbia; all the motets I ever remembered any part of; the texts in Stravinsky's *Symphony of Psalms,* which I sang often in a college chorus: all these texts were as new ones, each was a *shir hadash* or new song. I think particularly of just those lines from Psalm 40 in Stravinsky's setting:

Expectans exspectavi Dominum: & intendit mihi. Et exau-divit preces meas. . . . Et statuit supra petram pedes meos, & direxit gressus meos.

These were sung slowly and calmly, up through *preces meas,* the patience of "I waited patiently for the Lord; and he inclined unto me and heard my cry" expressed in the reduplication of *exspectans exspectavi* just as it is in the *kavo kiviti* of the Hebrew. The fugal texture gets denser and denser, the singers' own feet get "set upon a rock," and the music, as well as the Lord, are "establishing their goings." And then, after an instrumental interlude, the percussive force of the now homophonic texture at the words *Et immisit in os meum canticum novum. . . .* The familiar, old formulaic *shir hadash* of the Hebrew had never meant this, and any singer of the Stravinsky literally feels the presence of some kind of new song in his or her mouth at just that point in the setting. The composer's translation of the Latin has turned it into a praise of singing, even as the last section, with its setting of the *laudate eium in chordis et organo,* develops undertones of self-reference. But generally it was *singing* the Latin psalms, rather than listening to them, which brought yet another psalter into my possession.

Nor should I neglect my strange but nonetheless telling outsider's sense of the chanted psalms in the Book of Common Prayer. When young, I courted a young lady who sang in the choir of the college chapel, whose denomination was acutely Established, and I would often "to church repair / Not for the doctrine, but the music there" (as Alexander Pope disparagingly puts it, but which for me is always authenticating, the only true "doctrine" being music.)

John Hollander

I believe the reason that [the psalms] still have such a hold on us is because we're all still wandering through deserts, still crossing rivers, still walking through valleys of the shadow of death, still seeking promised lands.

William Ferris

Psalmody, which is native in Jewish and Christian liturgical worship, recedes as composed music expands.

The psalter was for centuries the liturgy's only hymnal because it was thought that the liturgy should consist solely in the celebration of God's Word in both written text and incarnational fulfillment. The liturgy was not viewed as scripture's step-child but as scripture's home. Musical hypertrophy, perhaps as much as any other factor, has been responsible for introducing tension between scripture and liturgy, rendering the relationship between all three problematic.

Many Church Fathers were aware of this early on, cautioning the churches about the power of virtuoso music to distract from the assembly's liturgical purpose.

Aidan Kavanagh

God has gone up with a shout,
   the LORD with the sound of a trumpet.
Sing praises to God, sing praises;
   sing praises to our king, sing praises.
For God is the king of all the earth;
   sing praises with a psalm.

Psalm 47:5–7

I shall sing a song of praise to God:
Strike the chords upon the drum.
God who gives us all good things —
Strike the chords upon the drum —
Wives, and wealth, and wisdom.
Strike the chords upon the drum.

Baluba, Zaire

ALL music is praise of the Lord, which some people cannot or will not understand, the real jazz form of a spiritual soil, is truly the musical psalms of the twentieth-century
man's torment in the tigerish growl of the trumpet. God's
wrath and mercy are in the demonic drumbeat and the milk-
smooth sound of the saxophone . . .

The Indian Express

THE Church knew what the Psalmist knew: Music praises
God. Music is well or better able to praise Him than the
building of the church and all its decoration; it is the Church's
greatest ornament.

Igor Stravinsky

So remember: just as the body of Jesus Christ was born by the Holy Spirit from the spotless Virgin Mary, so too the singing in the Church of God's praise, which is an echo of the harmony of heaven, has its roots in that same Holy Spirit. But the body is the garment of the soul and it is the soul which gives life to the voice. That's why the body must raise its voice in harmony with the soul for the praise of God. . . . God should be praised with crashing cymbals, with cymbals of clear praise and with all the other musical instruments that clever and industrious people have produced. For all the arts serving human desires and needs are derived from the breath that God sent into the human body. And that is why it is fitting that God be praised in all.

Hildegard of Bingen
Twelfth century

Hallelujah!

Praise! Praise God in the temple,
in the highest heavens!
Praise! Praise God's mighty deeds
and noble majesty.

Praise! Praise God with trumpet blasts,
with lute and harp.
Praise! Praise God with timbrel and dance,
with strings and pipes.

Praise! Praise God with crashing cymbals,
with ringing cymbals.
All that is alive, praise. Praise the Lord.

Psalm 150   Hallelujah!

SUDDENLY in a dream he saw a man standing beside him who called him by name. "Caedmon," he said, "sing me a song." "I don't know how to sing," he replied. "It is because I cannot sing that I left the feast and came here." The man who addressed him then said: "But you shall sing to me." "What should I sing about?" he replied. "Sing about the Creation of all things," the other answered. And Caedmon immediately began to sing verses in praise of God the Creator that he had never heard before, and their theme ran thus:

Praise we the Fashioner now of Heaven's fabric,
The majesty of his might and his mind's wisdom,
Work of the world-warden, worker of all wonders,
How he the Lord of Glory everlasting,
Wrought first for the race of men Heaven as a rooftree,
Then made he Middle Earth to be their mansion.

Bede
Eighth century

IT happened that there was a man named Augustine, a philosopher, later in his life a good Christian and an orthodox bishop, but who had been led astray by the errors of the Manicheans. He came to church one day in the wintertime, not out of interest in the sermon nor to see or hear the mystery of the Lord, but to refute and rebuke the blessed Ambrose, who was preaching and explaining to the people about the Lord's incarnation.

What happened, however, was that Augustine, forgetting both himself and all his philosophy, stood as if transfixed, pale and trembling in the sight of all who were there. Then, when the blessed Ambrose's charge to the people was done, Augustine came to see him in private. Now the Holy Spirit had made known to Ambrose all of Augustine's learning, and revealed to him all his education, and showed him in addition Augustine's excellence in logic, his points of difference with the true faith, and what a faithful and orthodox believer he would become. And so Ambrose received him very gently, and treated him with great kindness.

He rejoiced for Augustine like the father in the Gospel, who, embracing the son he had lost, weeping and placing his ring on his son's finger, kisses him, and then, reproaching his other son for his excessive envy, says to him, "Your brother was dead and now is alive again; he was lost and has been found." So with Augustine. A few days later, by the will of God, at the springs called St. John's, Augustine was finally baptized and confirmed by Ambrose, with God aiding him, in the name of the holy and indivisible Trinity. All the believers of the city stood by and watched, just as formerly many had watched him in his errors and agreed with him. And at these springs the Holy Spirit granted them eloquence and inspiration; and so, with all who were there hearing and seeing and marveling, they sang together the *Te Deum laudamus,* and so brought forth what is now approved of by the whole church, and sung devoutly everywhere.

Landulf of Milan
Eleventh century

TE deum," Lord, we sing;
We 'knowledge thee our King.

The whole wide world doth worship thee:
The Father of eternity.

To thee aloud all Angels cry:
The heav'ns and all the Pow'rs on high.

To thee, with never ending lay:
Cherub and Seraph sing and say:

All Holy is the Lord:
All Holy is the Lord.

Songs of Syon

Miles Davis

Don't play what's there, play what's not there.

O sing to the Lord a new song;
   sing to the Lord, all the earth.
Sing to the Lord, bless his name;
   tell of his salvation from day to day.
Declare his glory among the nations,
   his marvelous works among all the peoples.

Let the heavens be glad, and let the earth rejoice;
   let the sea roar, and all that fills it;
   let the field exult, and everything in it.
Then shall all the trees of the forest sing for joy
   before the Lord; for he is coming,
   for he is coming to judge the earth.
He will judge the world with righteousness,
Psalm 96:1–3, 11–13   and the peoples with his truth.

Leopold Stokowski

We are becoming the slaves of little marks on a piece of white paper which we call music.

I can't stand to sing the same song the same way two nights in succession. If you can, then it ain't music, it's close order drill or exercise or yodeling or something, not music.

Billie Holliday

THIS is, at first sight, an impossible precept. How can I sing a new song when all songs in all languages have already been sung time and time again to you, Lord? All themes are exhausted; all rhymes have been tried; all tunes have been explored. Prayer is essentially repetition, and I must struggle not to appear to say the same things every day, even when I know I am saying the same things. I am condemned to attempt variety even when I know well that all prayer reduces itself to the repetition of your name and the manifestation of my needs.

I know the answer before I finish the question. The song may be the same, but the spirit with which I sing it must be fresh and new every time. The zest, the joy, the sound of each word and the flight of each note has to be different every time that note leaves my lips, every time that prayer leaves my heart.

Carlos G. Valles

"SING unto the Lord a new song," the Psalter enjoins us again and again. It is the Christ-hymn, new every morning, that the family fellowship strikes up at the beginning of the day, the hymn that is sung by the whole Church of God on earth and in heaven, and in which we are summoned to join. God has prepared for Himself one great song of praise throughout eternity, and those who enter the community of God join in this song. It is the song that the "morning stars sang together and all the sons of God shouted for joy" at the creation of the world (Job 38:7). It is the victory song of the children of Israel after passing through the Red Sea, the Magnificat of Mary after the annunciation, the song of Paul and Silas in the night of prison, the song of the singers on the sea of glass after their rescue, the "song of Moses the servant of God, and the song of the Lamb" (Revelation 15:3). It is the new song of the heavenly fellowship.

Dietrich Bonhoeffer

A song does not exist until it is sung, or re-created, by a human voice. Every incarnation is different, and no one sound is the only right one. This is a paradox. A page of music seems to present a finished product, yet it contains no sound. (Hold it up to your ear: Can you hear it?) The song doesn't live until it comes off of the page and resumes its natural state as sound. The page can no more substitute for living sound than a recipe can for edible food.

Alice Parker

A LL things are wearisome;
      more than one can express;
the eye is not satisfied with seeing,
    or the ear filled with hearing.
What has been is what will be,
    and what has been done is what will be done;
    there is nothing new under the sun.
Is there a thing of which it is said,
    "See, this is new"?
It has already been,
    in the ages before us.
The people of long ago are not remembered,
    nor will there be any remembrance
of people yet to come
    by those who come after them.   Ecclesiastes 1:8–11

J. Bonnet
Eighteenth century

THE music of the church must be expressive . . . The passions of opera are cold in comparison to those of our church music.

Justine Ward

IF chant is not there to make me pray, let the cantors be silent. If chant is not there to appease my inner anxiety, let the cantors leave. If chant is not as valuable as the silence it breaks, let me go back to silence.

Eric Werner

THE acoustical beauty of a voice or of an instrument is usually described as "sweet," "agreeable," "strong." Hence, the purely aesthetic element in matters musical is not fully represented in Old Testament and early rabbinic literature; they either stress the social point ("agreeable"), or the sensual ("sweet"), or the majestic one.

Noel Coward

EXTRAORDINARY, how potent cheap music is.

N ow, brothers and sisters, if I come to you speaking in tongues, how will I benefit you unless I speak to you in some revelation or knowledge or prophecy or teaching? It is the same way with lifeless instruments that produce sound, such as the flute or the harp. If they do not give distinct notes, how will anyone know what is being played? And if the bugle gives an indistinct sound, who will get ready for battle? So with yourselves; if in a tongue you utter speech that is not intelligible, how will anyone know what is being said? For you will be speaking into the air. There are doubtless many different kinds of sounds in the world, and nothing is without sound. If then I do not know the meaning of a sound, I will be a foreigner to the speaker and the speaker a foreigner to me. So with yourselves; since you are eager for spiritual gifts, strive to excel in them for building up the church.

1 Corinthians 14:6–12

I f a song or a piece of music does not fulfill its ministerial function, it is better to be silent.

Lucien Deiss

T he dynamic nature of the worship event also suggests that the musical-liturgical-pastoral evaluation of the worship music must take into account the performance of the music in the liturgy, and not simply evaluate the music in its printed form. A common Western bias is that one can judge a composition according to what is in the score and, when appropriate, offer a separate judgment about the quality of the musicians or of the musical performance. When considering Christian ritual music, however, these judgments need to be fused. This fusion of the compositional and performative aspects of a piece is necessary because the quality of a work is influenced by its content.

Milwaukee Symposia
for Church Composers

THE stars of Balleymenone are the singers of the community's songs and the tellers of its tales. They lay no claim to original and creative genius. They are not the composers of their material but receive it from a tradition which links them with ancestors stretching back beyond memory. Generation after generation, stars have passed on stories of saints and heroes, of bandits and battles. The current stars feel a responsibility for the preservation of that tradition and, beyond that, for its interpretation. What they receive dare not be lost, but it may be — indeed *must* be — altered, embellished, rearranged, retold in such a way that facts transcend themselves in truth and the distant past interprets the emergent present.

Herman G.
Stuempfle, Jr.

I hear Great Grandmother singing,
singing as she always has and always will
for she is the sound of all that lives:
she is the breath of the Earth.
She is the weeping of sadness, sorrow,
      betrayal, treachery.
She is the voice of hope, joy, justice,
thunder of the ocean morning
of the river silence
of the cave wisdom
of the other shore.
I hear Great Grandmother singing,

Jewels on a String   singing through me.

FAIR the fall of songs
      When the singer sings them.
Still they are carolled and said —
      On wings they are carried —

Robert Louis
Stevenson
Nineteenth century

After the singer is dead
      And the maker buried.

I greatly desire that youth, which, after all, should and must be trained in music and other *proper* arts, might have something whereby it might be weaned from the love ballads and the sex songs and, instead of these, learn something beneficial and take up the good with relish, as befits youth. Nor am I at all of the opinion that all the arts are to be overthrown and cast aside by the Gospel, as some superspiritual people protest; but I would gladly see all the arts, especially music, in the service of Him who has given and created them.

Martin Luther
Sixteenth century

WE have to establish already in schoolchildren the belief that music belongs to everyone and is, with a little effort, available to everyone.

Zoltán Kodály

EDUCATION in music is most sovereign, because more than anything else rhythm and harmony find their way to the inmost soul and take strongest hold upon it, bringing with them and imparting grace, if one is rightly trained.

Plato
Fourth century BCE

Learn these tunes before you learn any others; afterwards learn as many as you please.

Sing them exactly as they are printed here, without altering or mending them at all; and if you have learned to sing them otherwise, unlearn it as soon as you can.

Sing all. See that you join with the congregation as frequently as you can. Let not a slight degree of weakness or weariness hinder you. If it is a cross to you, take it up, and you will find it a blessing.

Sing lustily and with a good courage. Beware of singing as if you were half dead, or half asleep; but lift up your voice with strength. Be no more afraid of your voice now, nor more ashamed of its being heard, than when you sang the songs of Satan.

Sing modestly. Do not bawl, so as to be heard above or distinct from the rest of the congregation, that you may not destroy the harmony; but strive to unite your voices together, so as to make one clear melodious sound.

Sing in time. Whatever time is sung be sure to keep with it. Do not run before nor stay behind it; but attend close to the leading voices, and move therewith as exactly as you can; and take care not to sing too slow. This drawling way naturally steals on all who are lazy; and it is high time to drive it out from us, and sing all our tunes just as quick as we did at first.

Above all sing spiritually. Have an eye to God in every word you sing. Aim at pleasing God more than yourself, or any other creature. In order to do this attend strictly to the sense of what you sing, and see that your heart is not carried away with the sound, but offered to God continually; so shall your singing be such as the Lord will approve here, and reward you when he cometh in the clouds of heaven.

John Wesley
Eighteenth century

LET us now sing the praises of
those who composed musical tunes,
   or put verses in writing;
all these were honored in their generations,
   and were the pride of their times.
Their bodies are buried in peace,
   but their name lives on
      generation after generation.
The assembly declares their wisdom,
   and the congregation proclaims their praise.

Sirach 44:1, 5, 7,
14–15

THE aim and final reason of all music should be nothing
else but the Glory of God and the refreshment of spirit.

Johann Sebastian Bach
Eighteenth century

I believe it's no good to talk about your songs; it's wrong.
You should leave your songs alone and let them say what
they say; let people take what they want from them.

Paul Simon

George Frideric
Handel
Eighteenth century

I did think I did see all Heaven before me and the great
God Himself.

Igor Stravinsky   THE Credo is the longest movement. There is much to believe.

Joseph Haydn
Eighteenth century   AT the thought of God [my] heart leapt for joy, and [I] could not help [my] music's doing the same.

O had I Jubal's lyre,
or Miriam's tuneful voice!
To sounds like his I would aspire,
Thomas Morell   in songs like hers rejoice!

Giovanni Pierluigi da
Palestrina
Sixteenth century   IF men take such pains to compose beautiful music for pro-fane songs, one should devote as much thought to sacred song, nay, even more than to mere worldly matters.

Charles Seeger   WE must, of course, be careful to avoid the fallacy that music is a universal language. There are many music-communities in the world, though not, probably, as many as there are speech communities. Many of them are mutually unintelligible.

Wнo is the Trinity?

You are music.
You are life.

Source of everything,
creator of everything,
angelic hosts sing your praise.

Wonderfully radiant,
deep,
mysterious.

You are alive in everything,
and yet you are unknown to us.

Hildegard of Bingen
Twelfth century

Wнеn long before time and the worlds were begun,
when there was no earth and no sky and no sun,
and all was deep silence and night reigned supreme,
and even our Maker had only a dream . . .

. . . the silence was broken when God sang the Song,
and light pierced the darkness and rhythm began,
and with its first birth-cries creation was born,
and creaturely voices sang praise to the morn.

To you, God the Singer, our voices we raise,
to you, Song Incarnate, we give all our praise,
to you, Holy Spirit, our life and our breath,
be glory for ever, through life and through death.

Peter Davison

PRAISE the living God who sings,
pulsing through created things,
harmonizing nature's arts,
voicing hope in human hearts!
Alleluia! Alleluia!
God's eternal anthem rings!
Alleluia! Alleluia!
Tell the nations God still sings!

Celebrate creation's God!
Magnify redemption's Lord!
Praise the Spirit's power to bring
understanding as we sing!
Alleluia! Alleluia!
Wake the woodwinds, pipes, and strings!
Alleluia! Alleluia!
David A. Robb   Join the anthem, God still sings!

FOR the music of creation,
for the song your Spirit sings,
for your sound's divine expression,
burst of joy in living things:
God, our God, the world's composer,
hear us, echoes of your voice —
music is your art, your glory,
Shirley Erena Murray   let the human heart rejoice!

O N the morning of the third day there was thunder and
lightning, as well as a thick cloud on the mountain,
and a blast of a trumpet so loud that all the people who
were in the camp trembled. Moses brought the people out
of the camp to meet God. They took their stand at the foot of
the mountain. Now Mount Sinai was wrapped in smoke,
because the LORD had descended upon it in fire; the smoke
went up like the smoke of a kiln, while the whole mountain shook violently. As the blast of the trumpet grew louder
and louder, Moses would speak and God would answer him
in thunder.　　　　　　　　　　　　　　　Exodus 19:16–19

A LL the others translate: the painter sketches
A visible world to love or reject;
Rummaging into his living, the poet fetches
The images out that hurt and connect,

From Life to Art by painstaking adaption,
Relying on us to cover the rift;
Only your notes are pure contraption,
Only your song is an absolute gift.

Pour out your presence, a delight cascading
The falls of the knee and the weirs of the spine,
Our climate of silence and doubt invading;

You alone, alone, imaginary song,
Are unable to say an existence is wrong,
And pour out your forgiveness like a wine.　　　　　　W. H. Auden

IN the darkness something was happening at last. A voice had begun to sing. It was very far away and Digory found it hard to decide from what direction it was coming. Sometimes it seemed to come from all directions at once. Sometimes he almost thought it was coming out of the earth beneath them. Its lower notes were deep enough to be the voice of the earth herself. There were no words. There was hardly even a tune. But it was, beyond comparison, the most beautiful noise he had ever heard. It was so beautiful he could hardly bear it. The horse seemed to like it too: he gave the sort of whinny a horse would give if, after years of being a cab-horse, it found itself back in the old field where it had played as a foal, and saw someone whom it remembered and loved coming across the field to bring it a lump of sugar.

"Gawd!" said the Cabby. "Ain't it lovely?"

Then two wonders happened at the same moment. One was that the voice was suddenly joined by other voices; more voices than you could possibly count. They were in harmony with it, but far higher up the scale: cold, tingling, silvery voices. The second wonder was that the blackness over-head, all at once, was blazing with stars. They didn't come out gently one by one, as they do on a summer evening. One moment there had been nothing but darkness; next moment a thousand, thousand points of light leaped out—single stars, constellations, and planets, brighter and bigger than any in our world. There were no clouds. The new stars and the new voices began at exactly the same time. If you had seen and heard it, as Digory did, you would have felt quite certain that it was the stars themselves who were singing, and it was the First Voice, the deep one, which had made them appear and made them sing.

"Glory be!" said the Cabby. "I'd ha' been a better man all my life if I'd known there were things like this."

The Voice on the earth was now louder and more triumphant; but the voices in the sky, after singing loudly with it for a time, began to get fainter. And now something else was happening.

Far away, and down near the horizon, the sky began to turn grey. A light wind, very fresh, began to stir. The sky, in that one place, grew slowly and steadily paler. You could see shapes of hills standing up dark against it. All the time the Voice went on singing.

There was soon light enough for them to see one another's faces. The Cabby and the two children had open mouths and shining eyes; they were drinking in the sound, and they looked as if it reminded them of something. Uncle Andrew's mouth was open too, but not open with joy. He looked more as if his chin had simply dropped away from the rest of his face. His shoulders were stooped and his knees shook. He was not liking the Voice. If he could have got away from it by creeping into a rat's hole, he would have done so. But the Witch looked as if, in a way, she understood the music better than any of them. Her mouth was shut, her lips were pressed together, and her fists were clenched. Ever since the song began she had felt that this whole world was filled with a Magic different from hers and stronger. She hated it. She would have smashed that whole world, or all worlds, to pieces, if it would only stop the singing. The horse stood with its ears well forward, and twitching. Every now and then it snorted and stamped the ground. It no longer looked like a tired old cab-horse; you could now well believe that its father had been in battles.

The eastern sky changed from white to pink and from pink to gold. The Voice rose and rose, till all the air was shaking with it. And just as it swelled to the mightiest and most glorious sound it had yet produced, the sun rose.

C. S. Lewis

You take the pen,
and the lines dance.
You take the flute,
and the notes shimmer.
You take the brush,
and the colours sing.
So all things have meaning and beauty
in that space beyond time where you are.
Dag Hammerskjöld   How, then, can I hold back anything from you?

To the Trinity be praise!
God is music, God is life
that nurtures every creature in its kind.
Our God is the song of the angel throng
and the splendor of secret ways
Hildegard of Bingen   hid from all humankind,
Twelfth century   But God our life is the life of all.

Notes

I am not satisfied: from *What Luther Says,* comp. Ewald M. Plass. Copyright © 1959, 1987 by Concordia Publishing House. Used with permission.

Siddhartha listened: from *Siddhartha* by Herman Hesse.

The English translation of Psalms 65, 92, 98, 126, 148, 150 and Isaiah 42 from The *Liturgical Psalter* © 1994, International Committee on English in the Liturgy, Inc. (ICEL); the English translation of discourse of St. Augustine on the psalms from *The Liturgy of the Hours* © 1974, ICEL; excerpts from the English translation of the General Instruction to the Roman Missal from *The Roman Missal* © 1973, ICEL; excerpts from the General Introduction of the *Order of Christian Funerals* © 1985, ICEL. All rights reserved.

Scripture texts are from the *New Revised Standard Version Bible,* © 1989, by the Division of Christian Education of the National Council of Churches of Christ in the United States of America. All rights reserved.

Illustrations by Fiona Hawthorne on pages i, iii, 1, 16, 43, 80, 92, 98, 107, 116, 145. All others from the Dover Pictorial Archive Series, *Catchpenny Prints,* and *Music: A Pictorial Archive of Woodcuts and Engravings.*

Together in the Realm of Sound

Singing is the most: from *Melodious Accord: Good Singing in Church* by Alice Parker, © 1991 Archdiocese of Chicago, Liturgy Training Publications.

Without music: from *Twilight of the Idols* by Friedrich Nietzsche, 1888.

But suddenly from out: from *Cry to Heaven* by Anne Rice, copyright © 1982 by Anne O'Brien Rice. Reprinted by permission of Alfred A. Knopf Inc.

Music leads us: from *The Insecurity of Freedom* by Abraham Joshua Heschel. Copyright © 1966 by Abraham Joshua Heschel and copyright renewed © 1994 by Sylvia Heschel. Reprinted by permission of Farrar, Straus & Giroux, Inc.

The year 1956: from *How I Changed My Mind* by Karl Barth, © 1966 by M. E. Bratcher. Published by John Knox Press.

Nothing is better: from *Master Teacher: Nadia Boulanger* by Don G. Campbell, © 1982. Published by The Pastoral Press.

We Need Each Other's Voice to Sing

We need each: from "We Need Each Other's Voice to Sing," by Thomas H. Troeger from *Borrowed Light,* © 1994 Oxford University Press, Inc. Reproduced by permission of the publisher.

The treasury of: from *Vatican Council II: The Conciliar and Post-Conciliar Documents,* ed. Austin Flannery, OP, © 1975. Published by Costello Publishing Company, Inc.

What is this: "What Is This Place," text © 1967, Gooi en Sticht, bv., Baarn, The Netherlands. All rights reserved. Exclusive agent for English-language countries: OCP Publications, Portland, OR. All rights reserved. Used with permission.

Bad music in church: from *Master Teacher: Nadia Boulanger* by Don G. Campbell, © 1982. Published by The Pastoral Press.

Augustine's commentary: from *The King of Instruments: How Churches Came To Have Organs* by Peter Williams, © 1993 by Peter Williams. Published in Great Britain by the Society for Promoting Christian Knowledge.

Considering issues of: from *The Milwaukee Symposia for Church Musicians,* © 1992, Archdiocese of Milwaukee. Copublished by National Association of Pastoral Musicians and Liturgy Training Publications.

One cannot find: from *Vatican Council II: The Conciliar and Post-Conciliar Documents,* ed. Austin Flannery, OP, © 1975. Published by Costello Publishing Company, Inc.

Harmonious Love

Therefore it is: from *The Apostolic Fathers,* ed. Jack N. Sparks, © 1978 by Thomas Nelson Inc., Publishers.

Heaven's not a place: From "Thoughts about heaven" in *An Anthology of the Love of God,* from the writings of Evelyn Underhill, © 1976. Reproduced by permission of Hodder and Stoughton Ltd.

Joyful, joyful: "Joyful, Joyful We Adore Thee," from *The Poems of Henry van Dyke,* © 1920. Reprinted with the permission of Scribner, a division of Simon & Schuster.

Music is sweet: "Music is sweet from the thrush's throat!" by E.E. Cummings, in *Complete Poems: 1904–1962*, ed. George J. Firmage. © 1973, 1991 by the Trustees for the E.E. Cummings Trust. Reprinted by permission of Liveright Publishing Corporation.

He who finds: from the preface to *The New England Psalm Singer.*

No sunset: "No sunset, but a grey, great, struggling sky" by E.E. Cummings, in *Complete Poems: 1904–1962*, ed. George J. Firmage. © 1973, 1991 by the Trustees for the E.E. Cummings Trust. Reprinted by permission of Liveright Publishing Corporation.

Ah, Lord: from #889, "Love for God," in The Oxford Book of Prayer, ed. George Appleton. © 1985 Oxford University Press.

Let All Things Their Creator Bless

All creatures: from "All Creatures of Our God and King" by William Draper, © 1923 (Renewed) by J. Curwen & Sons Ltd. All rights for U.S. and Canada controlled by G. Schirmer, Inc. (ASCAP). International copyright secured. All rights reserved. Reprinted by permission.

As I came: from *The Poetry of Robert Frost,* ed. Edward Connery Latham, © 1942 by Robert Frost, © 1970 by Lesley Frost Ballantine, © 1969 by Henry Holt and Company, Inc. Reprinted by permission of Henry Holt and Company, Inc.

Once in an: From "Missa Cantata" in *An Anthology of the Love of God,* from the writings of Evelyn Underhill, © 1976. Reproduced by permission of Hodder and Stoughton Ltd.

We probably derive: Gustav Mahler, quoted in Bauer-Lechner, *Recollections of Gustav Mahler,* 1980.

I shall take: from *Poetics of Music* by Igor Stravinsky, trans. Arthur Knodel and Ingolf Dahl, © 1942, 1947, 1970 by Harvard College.

Dear God: "The Prayer of the Little Bird," from *Prayers from the Ark* by Carmen Bernos de Gasztold, trans. Rumer Godden. Translation © 1962, renewed 1990 by Rumer Godden. Original © 1947, 1955 by Editions du Cloître. Used by permission of Viking Penguin Books USA Inc.

We cannot doubt: Eric Satie, quoted in John Cage, *Silence,* 1961.

The Angels Who Sing Glory

Let angels and: from "Helen's Hymn," by Sylvia Dunstan, © 1995 by GIA Publications, Inc.

The Cherubim: from *Apostolic Constitutions,* ed. F. X. Funk.

The Recording Angel: from *Themes and Conclusions* by Igor Stravinsky, 1972.

Where the bright: from "At a Solemn Musick" by John Milton.

The angels all: from *The Visions of Judgement* by Lord Byron, 1822.

A Vision of Eternity

The Apocalypse: from *The Bible and the Liturgy* by Jean Danielou, SJ, © 1956 by University of Notre Dame Press. Published by Servant Books.

For in Christ's: from *Poetical Works* by Edward Taylor, 1939.

Praise ought to be: from *Hildegard von Bingen's Mystical Visions* translated from *Scivias* by Bruce Hozeski. Copyright © 1986, Bear & Co., Santa Fe, NM. Reprinted with permission.

And the sound was: from *Hildegard von Bingen's Mystical Visions* translated from *Scivias* by Bruce Hozeski. Copyright © 1986, Bear & Co., Santa Fe, NM. Reprinted with permission.

Then, crowned again: from *Paradise Lost,* III, by John Milton.

Jerusalem, my happy: from "Jerusalem, My Happy Home," text by Joseph Bromehead. Public domain.

The air of: from *Hymns on Paradise* by St. Ephrem, trans. Sebastian Brock, © 1990. Reprinted by permission of St. Vladimir's Seminary Press, 575 Scarsdale Rd., Crestwood, NY 10707.

Musicians wrestle: from *The Poems of Emily Dickinson,* ed. Thomas H. Johnson, Cambridge, Mass.: Belknap Press of Harvard University Press. Copyright © 1951, 1955, 1979, 1983 by the President and Fellows of Harvard College.

The Clarity of the Source

Charlemagne too: from "Papal Schola versus Charlemagne," by S.J.P. van Dijk, in *Organica voces: Festschrift Joseph Smits van Waesberghe* (Institute voor Middeleeuwse Muziekwetenschap, 1963) trans. and adapt. in *Music in the Western World,* © 1984. Used by permission of Schirmer Books.

So far as: from *The Middle Ages,* vol. 2 of *The Christian Centuries* by David Knowles with Dimitri Obolensky, ©1969. Published by Paulist Press.

The challenge is: from *The Music of Silence* by David Steindl-Rast, OSB, with Sharon Lebell, © 1995. Published by HarperSanFrancisco.

The chastening: from *The Creators* by Daniel J. Boorstin, © 1992. Published by Random House.

With the understanding: from *Music and Worship in Pagan and Christian Antiquity* by Johannes Quasten. Reprinted by permission of The Pastoral Press.

The Thought that Fancied It

How all's to: "On a Piece of Music" from *The Poems of Gerard Manley Hopkins,* ed. W.H. Gardner. Published by Oxford University Press. Public domain.

The power of music: from *Copland on Music* by Aaron Copland, © 1955, 1956, 1960. Published by W. W. Norton & Company.

There is no real: Johannes Brahms, quoted in Gall, *Johannes Brahms,* 1961.

For the glory: Johannes Sebastian Bach, epigraph to *The Little Organ Book,* 1717.

I get up early: Joseph Haydn, quoted in Hughes, *Haydn,* 1970.

I haven't thought: from *Conversations with the Dead: The Grateful Dead Interview Book* by David Gans, ©1991. Published by Carol Publishing Group.

We must not: from *Contemporary Composers on Contemporary Music,* © 1967 by Elliott Schwartz and Barney Childs. Published by Holt, Rinehart and Winston.

Composers do not: Witold Lutostawski, quoted in Stucky, *Lutostawski and His Music,* 1981.

It Came from Above

Not from me: Joseph Haydn, quoted in Headington, *The Bodley Head History of Western Music,* 1974.

Although there are: from *Source Readings in Music History,* selected and annotated by Oliver Strunk. © 1950 by W. W. Norton Company, Inc.

If your talent: from *We Are Still Married: Stories & Letters* by Garrison Keillor, © 1982, 1989. Published by Viking Penguin Inc.

Rise, heart: from "No. 1 Easter" by George Herbert. Public domain. Can be found in *Five Mystical Sounds* published by Galaxy Music Corp.

Our priests: from "Icnocuicatl, Songs of Reflection." Reprinted from *Native Mesoamerican Spirituality,* ed. Miguel Leon-Portilla. © 1980 by the Missionary Society of St. Paul the Apostle in the State of New York. Used by permission of Paulist Press.

You should understand: from *The Syriac Fathers on Prayer and the Spiritual Life,* trans. Sebastian Brock. © 1987 by Cistercian Publications, Inc.

O black and: "O Black and Unknown Bards," from *Saint Peter Relates an Incident* by James Weldon Johnson. Copyright © 1917, 1921, 1935 by James

Weldon Johnson, copyright renewed © 1963 by Grace Nail Johnson. Used by permission of Viking Penguin Books USA Inc.

Blessed be you: "Blessed Be You, O God," by Thomas H. Troeger, from *Borrowed Light,* © 1994 Oxford University Press, Inc. Reproduced by permission of the publisher.

When the morning: "When the Morning Stars Together," by Albert F. Bayly, © 1969 by Oxford University Press. Used by permission.

Lord, how diverse: from *Choir Prayers* by Jeanne Hurt, © 1986. Used by permission of The Pastoral Press.

Music to Heav'n and Her We Owe

Your voices: Newburgh Hamilton, from "Alexander's Feast" by G.F. Handel.

In a garden: from "Anthem for St. Cecilia's Day," in *W. H. Auden: Collected Shorter Poems 1927–1957,* © 1966. Published by Random House.

While the clock: from *The Alteration* by Kingsley Amis, © 1976. Published by Carol & Graf Publishers, Inc.

With singing: from *Liber Usualis,* trans. Chris Comella.

From harmony: from "A Song for St. Cecilia's Day," by John Dryden, 1687.

In 1584: from *Dictionary of Christian Lore and Legend* by JCJ Metford. © 1983 Thames and Hudson Ltd.

Poetry Sung to Music

Etymologically, music: from "music" in *Dictionary of Word Origins* by John Ayto, © 1990. Published by Little, Brown & Company.

In the tradition: from *Celebration of the Word* by Lucien Deiss, CSSp, trans. Lucien Deiss and Jane M.-A. Burton. © 1993 by the Order of St. Benedict, published by Liturgical Press.

Let the word: Claudio Monteverdi, quoted in Morgenstern (ed.), *Composers on Music,* 1958.

Music is the: Henry Purcell, preface to *Diocletian, 1690.*

The setting to music: Francis Poulenc, quoted in Bernac, *Francis Poulenc,* 1977.

In order for: from *Foundations of Christian Music: The Music of Pre-Constantinian Christianity,* © 1992 GROW/Alcuin Publications.

For all its: from *The Insecurity of Freedom* by Abraham Joshua Heschel. Copyright © 1966 by

Abraham Joshua Heschel, copyright renewed © 1994 by Sylvia Heschel. Reprinted by permission of Farrar, Straus & Giroux, Inc.

Discard the Restricting Syllables

In addition to: from *Music in Catholic Worship,* copyright © 1983 United States Catholic Conference. Used with permission of the copyright owner. All rights reserved.

The wonderful thing: from *The Sufi Message of Hazrat Inayat Khan,* vol. 2, 2nd ed., London, 1973.

And so: Joseph Gelineau, quoted in *A More Profound Alleluia!: Gelineau and Routley on Music in Christian Worship* by Charles S. Pottie, SJ. Published by The Pastoral Press.

Marie did not: from *The Feast of All Saints* by Anne Rice, © 1979. Published by Simon & Schuster.

Perhaps, said Kretschmar: from *Doctor Faustus* by Thomas Mann, 1947, trans. Lowe-Porter.

My Beloved is: from *The Collected Works of St. John of the Cross,* trans. Kieran Kavanaugh and Otilio Rodriguez, © 1979, 1991 by Washington Province of Discalced Carmelites, ICS Publications, Washington, DC 20002-1199.

Measured by Silence

Once again: from *The Reed of God* by Caryll Houselander, © 1954, by Sheed and Ward.

Try as we may: from *Silence* by John Cage, 1961.

Nothing is more: from *Songs and Prayers from Taizé,* © 1991 Ateliers et Presses de Taizé. Published in the U.S. by GIA Publications, Inc.

In a sense: from *Man's Quest for God* by Abraham Joshua Heschel, © 1954; copyright renewed © 1982 Hannah Susannah Heschel and Sylvia Heschel. Published by Scribner's, an imprint of Simon & Schuster.

Some say one: from *Writings from the Philokalia on Prayer of the Heart,* trans. E. Kadloubovsky and G. E. H. Palmer. Published by Faber and Faber, Ltd.

To drop some: from *Sonnets from the Portuguese* by Elizabeth Barrett Browning, 1850.

In the ancient: from "The Silk Drum," by P.L. Travers. Reprinted from *Parabola: The Magazine of Myth and Tradition,* vol.V, no.2 (summer, 1980).

The notes I: Artur Schnabel, quoted in *Chicago Daily News,* 1958.

Quite spontaneously: Claude Debussy, letter to Chausson, 1893.

There's no music: from *Ethics of the Dust* by John Ruskin, 1886.

Let Anyone with Ears to Hear Listen

Oh Providence: Ludwig von Beethoven, postscript to the "Heiligenstadt Testament," 1802.

Great art: from *Memories and Commentaries* by Arnold Schoenberg, 1960.

A song that is: from *Psalms, Songs, and Sonnets* by William Byrd, 1611.

We hear too much: from *The Infinite Variety of Music* by Leonard Bernstein, 1966.

Any music you: from *Melodious Accord: Good Singing in Church* by Alice Parker. © 1991 Archdiocese of Chicago, Liturgy Training Publications.

The formation of: from *Theory of Sound* by Herman von Helmholtz, 1862.

Music is natural: from *The Path to the New Music* by Anton von Webern, 1960.

True music is for: from *Wilhelm Meister* by Johann Wolfgang von Goethe, 1796.

Those who maintain: from *Chronicles of My Life* by Igor Stravinsky.

Warble, child: from *Love's Labour's Lost,* III.i, by William Shakespeare.

Music is an: from *A General History of Music* by Charles Burney.

The Influence of Melodies

What tears I shed: from *The Confessions of St. Augustine,* trans. Rex Wagner, © 1963. Published by The New American Library, Inc.

Sometimes Francis: from *The Second Life of St. Francis* by Thomas of Celano.

A musical performance: from *Hildegard von Bingen's Mystical Visions* translated from *Scivias* by Bruce Hozeski. Copyright © 1986, Bear & Co., Santa Fe, NM. Reprinted with permission.

In truth we: from *The Geneva Psalter* by Jean Calvin, 1543.

There let the: from *Il Penseroso* by John Milton, 1645.

Music was as vital: from *The Story of Civilization* by Will Durant, 1937.

Music the fiercest: from "Ode for Musick, on St. Cecilia's Day," by Alexander Pope, c. 1708.

A Prodigious Incantation

Great music is: from *Shelburne Essays* by Paul Elmer More, 1910.

The tune came: from *The Collected Stories of Eudora Welty,* © 1936, copyright renewed © 1980 by Eudora Welty. Published by Harcourt Brace Jovanovich.

Presently, on the: from *Markheim* by Robert Louis Stevenson in *Christian Short Stories: An Anthology,* ed. Mark Booth, © 1984. Published by Crossroad Publishing Co.

Give me excess: from *Twelfth Night* by William Shakespeare, 1602.

She had never: from *Corelli's Mandolin* by Louis de Bernières, © 1995. Reprinted by permission of Vintage Books.

That which colours: Sanskrit proverb, quoted in Shankar, *My Music, My Life,* 1969.

Beauty Is Sacramental

Beauty is an: from *The Snowbird Statement on Catholic Liturgical Music,* © 1995, The Madeleine Institute.

The creative disbelief: from *The Singing Assembly,* vol. 6 of *Pastoral Music in Practice,* ed. Virgil C. Funk. Published by The Pastoral Press.

It is not the fact: from "There's Nothing Like a Professional Musician," by Robert Hovda in *Worship,* September 1986.

The pious in: from *Dissertation on Musical Taste* by Thomas Hastings, 1822.

Give thanks for: "Give Thanks for Music-Making Art," by Brian Wren. Words © 1993 by Hope Publishing Co., Carol Stream, IL 60188. All rights reserved. Used by permission of Hope Publishing Co., 800-323-1049.

Our limits: Robert Hovda, from National Association of Pastoral Musicians, 1982.

Musicians concerned: from "Preparing the Teacher to Meet the Challenge," an unpublished paper by Josephine Morgan, addressed to musicians at the time of Vatican II, in St. Louis.

Every sound: from *The Milwaukee Symposia for Church Musicians,* 1992, Archdiocese of Milwaukee. Copublished by National Association of Pastoral Musicians and Liturgy Training Publications.

June 12, 1980: by Chrysogonous Waddell in *Liturgy* magazine, published by Liturgical Conference. Used with permission.

Our society is: from *Melodious Accord: Good Singing in Church* by Alice Parker. © 1991 Archdiocese of Chicago, Liturgy Training Publications.

Making aesthetic: from *Music in Churches: Nourishing Your Congregation's Musical Life* by Linda J. Clark. © 1994 by Alban Institute.

In the past: from *Vision of Liturgy and Music for a New Century* by Lucien Deiss, trans. Jane M.-A. Burton. © 1996 by the Order of St. Benedict, published by Liturgical Press.

I Will Sing

What wondrous love: from "What Wondrous Love Is This," text by Alexander Means.

After Israel: from *Sing a New Song: The Psalms in the Sunday Lectionary* by Irene Nowell, OSB. © 1993 by the Order of St. Benedict, published by Liturgical Press.

There is delight: from "To Robert Browning" by Walter Savage Landor.

Sing God a simple: from "A Simple Song" by Leonard Bernstein and Stephen Schwartz © 1971. Reprinted by permission of Amberson Enterprises, Inc.

Singing is a noble: from *Table Talk* by Martin Luther, 1538.

Regular Moments, Recurring Moments

It is not: from *How Can I Keep from Singing?: Thoughts about Liturgy for Musicians* by Gabe Huck. © 1989 Archdiocese of Chicago, Liturgy Training Publications.

When we look: from *The Rites of People* by Gerard A. Pottebaum, © 1992. Published by The Pastoral Press.

Without a song: West African proverb, quoted in Roberts, *Black Music of Two Worlds,* 1973.

When music wakes: "When Music Wakes My Sleeping Heart," by Delores Dufner, OSB, copyright © 1991 by the Sisters of St. Benedict, 104 Chapel Lane, St. Joseph, MN 56374-0220. Used with permission.

'Tis a sure sign: from *The Maid of the Mill* by Isaac Bickerstaffe, 1765.

A Full, Rich, Human Celebration

We cannot be: from "There's Nothing Like a Professional Musician," by Robert Hovda in *Worship,* September 1986. Published by Liturgical Press.

Sacred music: from *Motu Propio,* St. Cecilia's Day, 1903, by Pope Pius X.

A theology of: from *The Milwaukee Symposia for Church Composers,* © 1992, Archdiocese of Milwaukee. Copublished by National Association of Pastoral Musicians and Liturgy Training Publications.

They affirmed: from a letter of Pliny the Younger to the emperor Trajan from the time when Pliny was the governor of Bithynia and Pontus (111 – 112).

O God: from "A Thansgiving for Music and Musicians" in *The Wideness of God's Mercy: Litanies to Enlarge Our Prayer,* vol. 1, by Jeffrey W. Rowthorn © 1985. Published by Winston Press.

Always Pointing to Christ

Liturgical music: Brother Roger of Taizé in conversation with Robert J. Batastini, October, 1983.

The Apostolic Age: from *Music and Worship in Pagan and Christian Antiquity* by Johannes Quasten, © 1983. Used by permission of The Pastoral Press.

But it is: from *Voices and Instruments in Christian Worship* by Joseph Gelineau, SJ, trans. Clifford Howell, SJ, © 1964. Published by Liturgical Press.

Beware the: Robert Hovda, from National Association of Pastoral Musicians, 1982.

Now we have: from *Shaw's Music* by Bernard Shaw, ed. Dan H. Laurence. © 1981, The Bodley Head Ltd.

When in our: "When in Our Music God is Glorified," by Fred Pratt Green. Words © 1972 by Hope Publishing Co., Carol Stream, IL 60188. All rights reserved. Used by permission of Hope Publishing Co., 800-323-1049.

Sing High, Sing Low

This holiest day: from "O Filii et Filiae," by Jean Tisserand, trans. John Mason Neale. Public domain.

Ours is a: from "Ours Is a Singing Faith," by Jane Parker Huber, © 1985, from *A Singing Faith,* © 1987. Used by permission of Westminster John Knox Press.

Therefore, let us: from *The Rule of Saint Benedict,* ed. and trans. Abbot Justin McCann. Published by Burns and Oates.

The joy it is: from *Tragic Psalms* by Francis Patrick Sullivan, © 1987. Used by permission of The Pastoral Press.

Sing my soul: "Sing My Soul, of Waking Life," by Becket Senchur, © 1994, World Library Publications, a division of J.S. Paluch Company, Inc. 3825 N. Willow Rd., Schiller Park, IL 60176. All rights reserved. Used by permission.

All Who Play the Lyre and Pipe

Descend ye: from "Ode to Musick, on St. Cecilia's Day," in *The Poems of Alexander Pope,* © 1963.

To You: from *Lyric Psalms* by Francis Patrick Sullivan, © 1983. Used by permission of The Pastoral Press.

As early as: from *Music & Worship in Pagan & Christian Antiquity* by Johannes Quasten, trans. Boniface Ramsey, OP. © 1973 National Association of Pastoral Musicians.

Soft sounds come: from *God's Image* by James Dickey and Marvin Hayes, © 1978 by Seabury Press.

With the Heart

Sing to God: from St. Jerome, commentary on Ephesians.

The man that: from "The Merchant of Venice" in *The Complete Works of William Shakespeare,* published by Doubleday. Public domain.

God guard me: from "A Prayer for Old Age" by William Butler Yeats, 1935.

Vide ut quod: from the blessing for liturgical musicians at the Fourth Council of Carthage (398).

There must be: Zoltán Kodály, preface to *Fifty-five Two-part Exercises,* 1954.

The Shorthand of Emotion

If one loves: from *Mr. Blue* by Myles Connolly, © 1928 by Macmillan Company, © 1954 by Doubleday & Company, Inc.

Israel's earliest: from *Finally Comes the Poet: Daring Speech for Proclamation* by Walter Brueggemann. © 1989 Augsburg Fortress.

My life flows: from "How Can I Keep from Singing?" adapted, with additional words, by Doris Plenn. © 1957 (renewed) by Sanga Music Inc. All rights reserved. Used by permission.

The Wall of the City Will Fall Down Flat

Through song: from *The Oath* by Elie Wiesel. © 1973 by Random House, Inc.

Some might say: from *How Can I Keep from Singing: Thoughts about Liturgy for Musicians* by Gabe Huck. © 1989 Archdiocese of Chicago, Liturgy Training Publications.

Quite in conformity: from *The Sacred Bridge* by Eric Werner. Published by Columbia University Press.

We need to: from *Hold Fast to Dreams: Writings Inspired by Zoltán Kodály* by Denise Bacon, © 1993. Published by Kodály Center of America.

People who: Paul Hindemith, quoted in Shapiro, *An Encyclopedia of Quotations about Music,* 1978.

The Words Themselves Sing

Let the words: from *Words that Sing* by Gail Ramshaw. © 1992 Archdiocese of Chicago, Liturgy Training Publications.

Several unhelpful: from *Words that Sing* by Gail Ramshaw. © 1992 Archdiocese of Chicago, Liturgy Training Publications.

How is it that: from *What Luther Says,* comp. Ewald M. Plass. Copyright © 1959, 1987 by Concordia Publishing House. Used with permission.

Those who choose: from *How Can I Keep from Singing: Thoughts about Liturgy for Musicians* by Gabe Huck. © 1989 Archdiocese of Chicago, Liturgy Training Publications.

Every place we: from *How Can I Keep from Singing: Thoughts about Liturgy for Musicians* by Gabe Huck. © 1989 Archdiocese of Chicago, Liturgy Training Publications.

One of the earliest: from *Music and Worship in the Church* by Austin C. Lovelace and William Rice. Rev. and enl. edition. Copyright © 1960, 1976 by Abingdon Press. Used by permission.

It is difficult: from *How Can I Keep from Singing: Thoughts about Liturgy for Musicians* by Gabe Huck. © 1989 Archdiocese of Chicago, Liturgy Training Publications.

A Genuine Expression

A psalm implies: from *Fathers of the Church,* vol. #46; *St. Basil: Exegetical Works,* trans. S Agnes Clare Way, © 1963. Used by permission of Catholic University of America Press.

Nobody can know: from "Psalms" by John Hollander in *Congregation: Contemporary Writers Read the Jewish Bible,* ed. David Rosenberg, © 1987 by Harcourt Brace & Company, reprinted by permission of the publisher.

I believe the: William Ferris in an interview with Alan Hommerding, May, 1995.

Psalmody, which is: from *Elements of Rite: A Handbook of Liturgical Style* by Aidan Kavanagh. © 1982, Public Publishing Company.

Sing a Song of Praise

I shall sing: from #1072 "Chords of Praise" in *The Oxford Book of Prayer,* ed. George Appleton, © 1985 Oxford University Press.

The Church knew: from *Conversations with Igor Stravinsky* by Igor Stravinsky and Robert Craft, © 1958.

So remember: from *Hildegard of Bingen's Book of Divine Works* by Matthew Fox. Copyright © 1987, Bear & Co., Santa Fe, NM. Reprinted with permission.

Suddenly in a: from *A History of the English Church and People* by Bede, trans. Leo Sherley-Price, revised by R. E. Latham, © 1955, 1968. Published by Penguin Books.

It happened that: originally from *Patrologiae cursus completus, Series Latina, CXLVIII* by Jacques Paul Migne. Translated to English by Lawrence Rosenwald for *Music in the Western World,* © 1984 by Schirmer Books. Used by permission of Lawrence Rosenwald.

Te Deum: from "Te Deum Laudamus," in *Songs of Syon.* Public domain.

Play What's Not There

We are becoming: Leopold Stokowski, quoted in Jacobson, *Reverberations,* 1975.

I can't stand: from *Lady Sings the Blues* by Billie Holliday, 1956.

This is, at first: from *Psalms for Contemplation* by Carlos G. Valles, SJ. © 1990 Loyola University Press.

Sing unto the Lord: from *Life Together* by Dietrich Bonhoeffer, trans. John W. Doberstein. © 1954 by Harper & Row Publishers.

A song does not: from *Melodious Accord: Good Singing in Church* by Alice Parker. © 1991 Archdiocese of Chicago, Liturgy Training Publications.

The Passions of Opera Are Cold

The music of: from *Histoire de la Musique* by J. Bonnet, 1725.

If chant is not: from *Justin Ward and Solesmes* by Pierre Combe, © 1987, Catholic University of America Press.

The acoustical beauty: from *The Sacred Bridge* by Eric Werner, © 1959, Columbia University Press.

Extraordinary, how: from *Private Lives* by Noel Coward, © 1947 by Samuel French.

If a song: from *Visions of Liturgy and Music for a New Century* by Lucien Deiss, trans. Jane M.-A. Burton. © 1996 by the Order of St. Benedict, published by Liturgical Press.

The dynamic nature: from *The Milwaukee Symposia for Church Composers,* © 1992, Archdiocese of Milwaukee. Copublished by National Association of Pastoral Musicians and Liturgy Training Publications.

Back Beyond Memory

The stars of: from *Images of Ministry: Reflections of a Seminary President* by Herman G. Stuempfle, Jr. © 1995 by CSS Publishing Company, Inc.

Fair the fall: from *Songs of Travel* by Robert Louis Stevenson, 1896.

Learn Something Beneficial

I greatly desire: from *What Luther Says,* comp. Ewald M. Plass. Copyright © 1959, 1987 by Concordia Publishing House. Used with permission.

We have to establish: Zoltán Kodály, lecture, 1946.

Education in music: from *The Republic* by Plato.

Learn these: from *Select Hymns* by John Wesley, 1761. Public domain.

The Pride of Their Times

I did think: George Frideric Handel, attr., quoted in Lang, *Georg Frideric Handel,* 1967.

The Credo is: Igor Stravinsky, quoted in Machlis, *Introduction to contemporary Music,* 1963.

At the thought: Joseph Haydn, quoted in Hughes, *Haydn,* 1970.

O had I: Thomas Morell, from the oratorio "Joshua" by G. F. Handel.

If men take: Giovanni Pierluigi da Palestrina, preface to *First Book of Motets,* 1563.

We must, of course: from "Music and Culture" by Charles Seeger, 1941.

You Are Music

Who is the Trinity: from *Meditations with Hildegard of Bingen,* Gabrielle Uhllen. Copyright © 1983, Bear & Co., Santa Fe, NM. Reprinted with permission.

When long before: partial text from "The Singer and the Song," by Peter Davison (vv. 1, 2, 6).

Praise the living: from "Praise the Living God Who Sings," by David A. Robb, © 1984, Selah Publishing Co., Inc. Kingston, NY 12401. All rights reserved. Used by permission.

For the music: from "For the Music of Creation," Shirley Erena Murray. Words © 1992 by Hope Publishing Co., Carol Stream, IL 60188. All rights reserved. Used by permission of Hope Publishing Co., 800-323-1049.

All the others: from "The Composer" in *W. H. Auden: Collected Shorter Poems 1927–1957,* © 1966. Published by Random House.

In the darkness: from *The Magician's Nephew* by C.S. Lewis. Reprinted by permission of HarperCollins Pubishers, London.

You take the pen: from *Markings* by Dag Hammarskjold, trans., Auden/Sjoberg. Copyright © 1964 by Alfred A. Knopf Inc. and Faber & Faber Ltd. Reprinted by permission of Alfred A. Knopf.

To the Trinity: from St. Hildegard of Bingen *Symphonia: A Critical Edition of the Symphonia armonie celestium revelationum,* ed. and trans. Barbara Newman. Copyright © 1989 by Cornell University. Used by permission of the publisher, Cornell University Press.

Author/Source Index